Mother Lover
Woman Warrior
Embracing Perfect Imperfection

Kiley Baker

First published by Busybird Publishing 2016
Copyright © 2016 Kiley Baker

ISBN
Print: 978-0-9945728-2-0
Ebook: 978-0-9945728-3-7

Kiley Baker has asserted her right under the Copyright, Designs and Patents Act 1988 to be identified as the author of this work. The information in this book is based on the author's experiences and opinions. The publisher specifically disclaims responsibility for any adverse consequences, which may result from use of the information contained herein. Permission to use information has been sought by the author. Any breaches will be rectified in further editions of the book.

All rights reserved. No part of this publication may be reproduced, stored in or introduced into a retrieval system, or transmitted in any form, or by any means (electronic, mechanical, photocopying, recording or otherwise) without the prior written permission of the author. Any person who does any unauthorised act in relation to this publication may be liable to criminal prosecution and civil claims for damages. Enquiries should be made through the publisher.

Cover image: Emma Wise Photography
Cover design: Busybird Publishing
Layout and typesetting: Busybird Publishing
Editor: Jodie Garth

Busybird Publishing
2/118 Para Road
Montmorency Victoria
Australia 3094
www.busybird.com.au

Testimonials

The first time I saw Kiley fight, I thought to myself, 'What a warrior.' She's small in structure but has a huge heart and I was very fortunate to train with her for 8 years. Kiley taught me a lot. Kiley, now a single mother of three kids, is running a full-time karate school by herself. To me, she defines the phrase 'Never give up!' She is a terminator; she is a rock!

– Shihan Judd Reid
Original Uchi Deshi (live-in) student under Sosai Mas Oyama, star of the movie 100 Man Fight, WKO Champion, and author of the soon to be released Young Lions

I have trained with Kiley for over 4 years. During that time, she has helped me improve not only the physical aspects of health, including recovering from injury, but the mental as well. She has helped to improve my self-confidence and mental toughness. Kiley has created a community in her dojo – we train hard, but we support and encourage each other. There is no elitism; the dojo is social and, although it appears understated and humble, it is very powerful and positive, much like the lady herself!

– Elise Burl
Martial arts student and personal training client

I have known Kiley for 14 years, since my first son joined her dojo at the age of 8. I reflect on how she has helped to shape the man he is today, now 21. Kiley is passionate about health and well-being and is encouraging, disciplined and genuine. There is no doubt her experience and commitment has kept our family coming back for more gruelling workouts. We owe our fitness level to you, Kiley. Thank you.

– **Judy Cheng**
Mmartial arts student and mother of three boys

Kiley has been my personal trainer for approximately a year now. I started the program with the intention of losing weight whilst learning some defence moves. Kiley has certainly helped me achieve both, but has also empowered me to be more confident about myself. Now I know that this was Kiley's intention all along!

– **Joanne Kelso**
Personal training client and mother of two

Kiley has taught me so much about discipline and the need to respect everyone and everything around me. She has taught me that even though she is little, it doesn't mean anyone should ever underestimate her, and that little people can make a big impact. The time and effort she put into me alone was incredible. For someone to show so much belief in me and my abilities was a huge confidence boost for someone who got bullied and put down by others.

–**Daniel Wilcox**
Former student as a child, now studying to be a teacher

I have trained with Kiley for close to a decade now. When I started, I was overweight and out of shape. Now, even though I train 5 days a week with her, it is never boring. She finds a way to keep things fun, all the while sharing the wisdom she has gleaned through the years.

– **Mark Niven**
Student and assistant instructor

This book is dedicated to my three little munchkins, Thaila, Deshan and Sanjay. Please remember that I love you unconditionally – always.

I hope that I've shown you why it's so important to work hard and strive for your dreams, and that you all grow up to do just that – even better than I have!

It is also dedicated to my students (past, present and future). Without you, I couldn't have begun to pass on all that I've learned and gained through my time in martial arts and fitness. You give me strength and courage.

Contents

Introduction	i
Mother	1
Mother is Born	2
Chapter 1 – A New Mum is Born	3
Chapter 2 – Kids: Kryptonite for Supermums	15
Chapter 3 – Nobody Told Me That	23
Lover	33
I was She	34
Chapter 4 – Where Did My Sexy Go?	35
Chapter 5 – It's Not Me, It's Them	43
Chapter 6 – Separation Anxiety	53
Woman	63
The Mighty Queen	64
Chapter 7 – I Am Woman	65
Chapter 8 – Perfect Imperfection	73
Chapter 9 – Because You're Worth It!	87
Chapter 10 – Designing Destiny	93
Warrior	101
Fighting	102
Chapter 11 – Warrior Training	105
Chapter 12 – Who's in Your Corner?	117
Chapter 13 – It's Not About the Belt	127
Afterword	139
About the Author	140
I Am Woman Programs	142
Special Book Offer	143
Kiley Baker – As a Speaker	144
I Am Woman Online	146

Introduction

Last night I went to my first buck's night. Yes, that's right – me, a woman, going to a buck's night. You might be wondering why I was even asked to attend. Well, I actually requested to go along as I thought it might be fun. And I was right. I had a great time!

Now, I can't speak for all buck's parties and hen's nights – so can only compare the stories I hear and those that I've actually attended – but I would say buck's parties are often less sexually charged than a hen's night. The guests are probably more drunk and perhaps crude and silly and, no doubt, there is a stripper element, etc., but, nevertheless, I think women can go really feral crazy on such nights.

I wonder if that's because it's kind of socially accepted that men will, on occasion, hit the turps, go clubbing and end up wandering into a strip club at regular intervals throughout their adult life. For a woman, however, this type of behaviour is generally reserved for hen's nights and perhaps 40th birthday parties and it's expected for them to go all out crazy when that day finally arrives. There's a whole study in itself right there.

But, let's get back to my role on the night. Why was I actually there? Personally, I love going to strip clubs and watching women take their clothes off, dance seductively and mesmerise men of all types.

It might be strange to hear this from a heterosexual woman with three kids, but it's the truth. There is definitely the aspect of it being naughty, which makes it appealing. But for me, I don't find the atmosphere so sleazy, but rather a fun, carefree, 'anything goes' type of feeling. I dare say there are sleazy clubs out there but, fortunately for me, I don't think I've attended any of those to date. (One night in Thailand will be made an exception). Of course, most of the women are attractive, but it's the different types of body shapes, hair styles, images and attitudes of these women that I like to see. As females, I think we have this perception of the ideal woman. The skinny body shape, big breasts, long blonde hair and blue eyes that we think all men will be attracted to.

What I find interesting about the clubs is that this is not always the case. Some men gravitate to the small girls; others to the smoking red head with the air of attitude. Some to the voluptuous girl with curves to spare and then, of course, the varieties of colours and races and dance styles. For me, it reaffirms that we are all different and somewhere out there is someone who likes a woman that looks like me.

I also see it as a bit of a power play for women and that it's them who are in control of the scene here. It may be an illusion, but I don't really care, as that's part of the game. Part of the fun and part of the attraction. All women, I believe, at their innermost core would like to be in control of their sexuality. They want to be visually appealing to their mate, desired and wanted, but they also want to be able to decide when they want to be sexual and when they want to be just held, because they are who they are.

Introduction

What woman doesn't want to be able to turn on a man when she wants to? Of course, naked bodies aren't the only thing that turns men on. Everyone's different. Some men love a woman who cooks and some love a woman in uniform and others get turned on by their pregnant mate or the one outside working the chainsaw. I don't think I'm guessing when I say that at some point the stimulus is visual – it's just these aesthetic qualities change depending on the preferences of the person.

After having told a few people that I was going along for the party, it dawned on me that it wasn't really accepted by all that it was something I actually wanted to do. They thought, perhaps, that I just wanted to be cool or I wanted attention. But, I'm sorry, that couldn't be further from the truth. I have always preferred the company of male friends and, growing up, the mates at school whom I got along well with were mostly males.

Of course, I have had a few special female friends and they know who they are but, for the most part, I find I don't always have a lot in common with other females and I find the gossip and mental games which sometimes come with female friendships torture. At least with a male friend, they tell you straight up if you're annoying them or if they're angry at you or don't want to hang out with you, etc. You can tell each other to eff off and get over it and the following day hang out again and all is cool. Not with a girlfriend – not so easy. Going out with a group of guys hell-bent on having a good time, no pressure, and able to just be me sounded like a great idea. No ulterior motives to my knowledge … or were there?

Once people began to question me, I started to ask myself whether the reason I started going to the strip clubs was some kind of self-torture. Some type of self-destructive behaviour that seemed to fit some of the negative parts of my profile? Was I pretending to be okay with this scene in an effort to prove to everyone, including myself, that I had accepted me for me? My body and my sexuality? Hmm … These are all important questions, and timely at that.

Considering I had just come out of an 11-year relationship with the father of my children and found myself single, trying to run my business 5 days per week on top of an office job 3 days per week and still struggling financially, I was starting to question everything. What was I really made of, and what did I want to achieve?

'Geez, who am I anyway?' I asked myself. That's when I realised that I was trying so hard to be everything to everyone: a mother to my children – and I wanted to be a great one. A lover whom a man would appreciate enough to keep. A woman who was comfortable with herself. A warrior who taught and motivated others. A business owner and someone who never backed down.

Many people go on a quest to find themselves. They go on a trip overseas or delve into nature, meditation or a new hobby or perhaps abandon their current lives in the search for another that they hope will more closely match their inner qualities. I had read the book Eat, Pray, Love by Elizabeth Gilbert a few years earlier and it was popping back into my head now that these questions were confronting me. I loved that book and it resonated with me on so many levels, but I was just not in a position to drop everything and take myself away on an extended overseas trip like the author did in that.

I didn't have the money and I did have the children whom I couldn't just step away from. Even if, perhaps, I needed to. Besides, my belief is that of course one can 'find themselves' in the middle of Italy eating ice cream and pasta, or indeed get in touch with their true essence whilst meditating in the silence of a forest with no interruptions or distractions. It's holding onto that identity and that feeling in the middle of the chaos we call life. That is our challenge.

See, I thought I knew who I was. I was Kiley Baker. Now 40 years old, mother of three beautiful kids, martial arts instructor, potential partner and a woman … and I am all of those things, but they describe what I am physically and what I do, but not who or what I am at my core. That is our quest in life, isn't it? To know who we actually are? And why we are here and how we are to contribute to the world?

I put forward the proposition that none of us are put here for just one major reason. We're here to touch many lives, to play various roles, to grow and change, and in doing all of these things perhaps discover some wisdom that we may pass onto our children, friends, colleagues, or others who are on this same journey. I'm not even sure that one needs to be aware of what all these things are, but to be mindful of the process and accepting of oneself along the way. In the end, does it really matter if you don't know the answer to the big 'why' or 'what'? Perhaps what is important is only that you did indeed live, and how.

So, how can we live better?

In this book, I will share with you my experiences so far on my personal journey, in the hope that any wisdom I have garnered over the last 40 years may be of some interest and help to you. Perhaps the insights I now have will help you to live better, or they may just simply make you feel more comfortable as you realise that you aren't alone on your journey.

I ask that you 'use' this book. Don't just read it and then put it back on the shelf to gather dust. Stick tabs and notes on any pages that you find useful. Scribble on the pages and highlight the words that gel with you. Tear out bits if you have to, but don't just let the words wash over you if the subject matter resonates. Too often, I've read amazing things and then forgotten where it was to find again. Now, I take photos with my phone or write it on my chalkboard in my kitchen. Keep information that you want to influence you in your face, if you want it to permeate your life and make a difference.

As you go through the book, you will see that I end each chapter with the word 'Osu'. It is pronounced 'oss' and should be stated with confidence. This is a saying that we use often in my style of karate and almost becomes a spiritual term for us that isn't just said but is felt. Later, in Chapter 10, I will go through the deeper meaning of the word and by then, through reading, perhaps it will become clearer. In its essence, when we recite this, it is a form of respect to our instructor, but more so a pledge to ourselves that we will never give up. When you read it, say it strong in your mind or, even better, say it aloud. It might feel funny at first – but everything new feels awkward in the beginning. If you want to change your life, get comfortable being out of your comfort zone. Osu.

I hope you are as excited about reading this book as I am to be writing it. So, with great pleasure and without further ado … Hajime! (That's 'begin' in Japanese.)

Mother

Mother is Born

In what I perceived to be an instant, despite months in preparation,

My very existence changed.

My heart began to overflow and everything inside me shifted;

The fabric of my life was rearranged.

There you were, this tiny specimen of innocence and truth –

No flaws, no faults, so soft to me; perfect.

The fear I felt just hours before had all but vanished now;

My instinct switched to nurture and protect.

I stared with wonder, as you slept, at this miracle of life

And I pinched myself to see if this was true.

I prayed my love would be enough to steer you right and keep you safe.

The universe had gifted me an angel dressed up as you.

Chapter 1

A New Mum is Born

The moment a child is born, the mother is also born. She never existed before. The woman existed, but the mother never. A mother is something absolutely new.
— **Raj Nish**

Picture the Earth Mother. Clean, un-styled hair, natural and minimal makeup, calm, collected and softly spoken and unfazed by small dilemmas such as dirty clothes, a cough or a cold or the lost car keys. When Earth Mother moves about, she seems to float and a soft glow encompasses her and when she enters the room with her beautifully behaved children, the energy in the room lightens and everyone is happy to see her. Prior to giving birth, this is how I envisioned myself as a mother. I had plans to never be that mum, shouting at the kids in the supermarket or barking orders at my children.

No, I was going to be lovely. I'm embarrassed to say that this vision came crashing down about 6 hours after my first-born daughter came into the world. Of course, I love my children with all my heart, with all that I have to the ends of the earth. I distinctly remember, however, being disappointed that neither I nor my new baby were this perfect vision when, on that first night in the hospital, she wouldn't sleep and neither could I.

I was more upset with myself than with her. I wanted to stay awake and watch her tiny little chest move as she breathed. This precious little package of mine looked so fragile and so dependent. I wanted to instantly protect her, but I also really wanted to sleep. I was exhausted. I had actually gone into labour, waters broken but no constant contractions, almost 48 hours before, so I had hardly slept since then. I was anxious to meet my daughter and I had wanted to have an all-natural water birth, which I would not have been able to have, had she not come of her own accord when she did.

I think I tried everything to bring the labour on. Walking, both flats and up the massive hills which surrounded our house in the Dandenong Ranges back then. Hot spicy food, shopping, sex and anything else that anyone suggested. However, the final push in the right direction came from the painful but effective stretch and sweep from my lovely midwife and then 9 hours later, after a drug-free water birth, she was here.

This is not one of those books where I pull out all the gross details of my labour. We each have our stories and they are wonderful and awful and painful and amazing and most of them end in joy and a baby in our arms. If that is the case, then we as mothers are the witnesses of miracles and are lucky beyond measure.

Now, to remember and hold onto that feeling as we walk

into the brand new world of being a mother. It's been said before that children should come with a manual. Your midwives provide assistance in the first few hours and the local health nurses all have helpful tips, but only if you are lucky enough to get a good one. I must say, I feel fortunate to have had pleasant experiences in this area. However, I think it's a shame that nowadays we are all so busy living separate lives that we don't have the support of the extended family on hand. Not always. There are plenty of books out there to help you with the 'what to do' bits, but it is not so easy to find a book which tells you about all the crazy emotions you might go through.

Why didn't someone tell me that there may come a day when I would be so tired, so exhausted, feel so isolated and lonely at home with this new baby, that I would get angry with this screaming thing that won't shut up no matter how many times I feed her or rub her back or hold her this way, or rock her, or swaddle her, or go outside, or carry or bathe her or change her nappy or … aargh. No one was honest enough to say that it's okay to want to put a pillow over her face to stop the crying for merely a minute, but just don't. Of course I never did, but I did think that there was something wrong with me for getting angry with my little girl and getting so disappointed at feeling like that. I felt like a bad mother.

As I explained earlier, illusion shattered. I remember once pushing the bassinet all the way down to the other side of the house, closing all the doors behind me and going to sit outside, crying. I called my then partner on the phone and told him what was happening. Fortunately for me, he handled it well and told me I'd done the right thing to take time out and calm down and to go back inside the house. He assured me that baby would be fine and she would settle soon. And eventually we both did, but I hadn't been prepared for these feelings of helplessness at not being able to settle my own baby. Again, I just wanted to be picture perfect. I wanted my baby to always be content and happy and sleeping and clean and beautiful. But mine had uncontrollably cried. And so had I.

A statistic from PANDA, the association for Perinatal Anxiety and Depression Australia, released figures that 1/7 mothers and 1/10 fathers experience postnatal depression. They are pretty alarming numbers. I don't believe I ever suffered from postnatal depression or significant problems relating to becoming a new mother or even a second- or third-time mother. However, I think that existing in the realm of 'normal' can still be an immense struggle. Nobody writes books about the normal people. It's actually become fairly socially acceptable now – and this is a good thing – to sit on the far ends of the spectrum. To be the superhuman power mum, the always smiling organic earth mother or, at the opposite end of the line, the mother with depression. You can find praise, help, understanding or information anywhere if you're one of those people. It's almost alienating, however, to admit that yeah, you're doing okay, but something just isn't quite right.

As families get closer on social media but further apart physically and emotionally, we often portray our lives online as more than they are. Here's a picture of my beautiful baby, immaculate and smiling, all sleeping soundly, all swaddled up. What people don't see is the 85 pics you took of the baby struggling to get out of your arms, crying, whinging and then pooping halfway up their shoulders again and not sleeping for 5 hours and breast feeding every 2 and all you want is a second's peace so you can have a shower after you crawl your way through the mess on the floor just to get to the bathroom. What they don't see, either, is the photo of you passed out on the sofa with breast milk squirting all over your child's face, and they don't see the argument you just had with your partner because of the smallest thing. It's easy to see the perfect pictures online and wonder why your life isn't like that too. Well … it's because theirs isn't really like that, either.

I'm not making light of mums who do suffer from depression. They need help and understanding, but so do the mums who are just coping. I guess I'm trying to say that we are new to this job, we are all on a hormonal roller coaster, deprived of sleep, trying to do our best and wondering if we are even doing a good job. We are all nervous and unsure and at times we feel isolated and alone and I really do think that, for the most part, it's normal. I believe I can say, looking back now, that it was okay to feel like that. Despite sometimes not being a picture of perfection, we had some pretty amazing moments mixed in with the confusion and the occasional negative emotions.

Overall, I had a wonderful first year at home with my little princess. We went for walks and to mothers' groups and shopping together and I treasured the nights when we did fall asleep on the bed together, especially after feeding, as it was great bonding. I loved waking up and seeing her curled up beside me, arms in the air and looking like a peaceful little angel that was cute enough to squeeze. I love the times when she would do something new: smiling, rolling over and eventually sitting up all by herself, crawling, then talking and walking. Each milestone was filled with praise with love from Mummy and Daddy and I was always in awe of how amazing she was.

And I was proud. It felt to me like I was learning and experiencing right along with her. I was growing too. I was actually seeing life and the world around me through different eyes. I didn't have them before, because they were hers and she was sharing them with me. I then got to have similar experiences with each of my two boys. Of course, each pregnancy, birth, baby and child is different. The stories then are not the same for all of them. However, what is the same is that feeling of love a mother has for her child and each time I think the mother is reborn also.

I often wonder … why do we become mums? The hardest job of all? One reason, I guess, is because you get to be you, only better. There's more of you now. In fact, there's a smaller version of you and you get to work with this little person. Only a mother can know that love, that all-enveloping, all-encompassing, you-have-no-control-over-it type of love. People can talk about it, but until it happens to you and you experience it for yourself, I don't think you really know the extent of that love, that … something. I guess the pay sucks, but the job satisfaction is amazing.

I mean, you can't really put a numerical value on the time that you spend as a mother with your children. If we use child support payments or payments from the government for a stay at home mum as a gauge, I don't think they can even begin to financially renumerate the work that a mother does at home. But at the end of the night, after your long hours in the office, if that's what you want to call it, when you put the children to bed, the job satisfaction feels great. You kiss them on the forehead and even if you've had a bad day, you look forward to them waking up and doing it all again.

There is a famous quote from 1964 by the founding mothers of La Leche League International. It says, 'As a woman grows in mothering, she grows as a human being and every other role she may fill in her lifetime is enriched by the insights and humanity she brings to it from her experiences as a mother.' I honestly believe that that's true. Everything we do from then on in is changed. I know, for myself, I can't watch a movie the same way that I used to before having children, especially if something in the movie happens to a child. The connection that I feel to that happening is different because I now have a child of my own and I can place myself, or indeed my child, into that situation.

I think, also, we become a little bit more nurturing, and we bring that nurturing into other areas of our life as well. For example, I know my teaching has changed a lot because I now understand kids a little better and this has meant my instruction of the junior class has changed. My patience is different – at times it's worse, but often it is better – but it has made a difference to the way I instruct the adults, too.

Becoming a mother is not just about giving birth to a child, although that's how it's often described in the dictionary – that you are the female parent. Being a mother is about sharing love and affectionate care, teaching and guiding, bringing up and raising a child. Becoming a mother is often also about being the head of a community and the community, in this instance, is your family.

Some women might worry about, or are perhaps afraid of, becoming a mum. Fearful that they won't know what to do. Well … you don't need to worry. You will be given instincts. There is something real about a mother's instinct and your job, I believe, is to listen to those. We can take advice from other mothers in a position to offer us guidance because they're more educated in a particular area, or your mother's been a mother, so she knows, but at the same time there is a deep connection between a mother and her child and that is something that you should listen to. If your gut tells you that your child is sick, often you know well before the child is really displaying symptoms and that's just something that mums know. I think it's really important that you remember that you're given those instincts for a reason and to use them to help you as they're your inherent guides. You have the tools and often, as a new parent, you sit there and find yourself saying things that your parents said and even though you might cringe, this is your learning coming down that you can now pass onto others.

Filter this passed-on information, by all means, but the tools are there. You will have them. You have your own life experience too. You have your own mistakes to learn from, and your successes to talk about with and show to your children. You will be proud of your kids and you will encourage them and you will push them and, sure, it might not be the right way every time but I'm pretty sure that your intentions will be honourable and good and will only come from love. So don't panic. You have the ability. It's there; it's intrinsic.

Some people say, 'What if I don't turn out to be a great mum?' Well … nobody can know that in advance and neither can anyone prepare you. Motherhood brings out all of your strengths. Stuff inside yourself you never even knew you had. Sure, it might bring out some of your weaknesses as well, and they're things you can build on and create new strengths with.

Then some might say, 'What if they aren't my children by birth?' Perhaps you've entered into a new relationship with someone who already has children of their own. You didn't give birth to these little people. But as we mentioned before, becoming a mother is not just about giving birth but it's about raising and showing affectionate care and love and you have the ability to show the children who are under your care these things. So, in many ways you take on a motherly role even if you aren't the biological mother. That is still possible and you're still allowed to have all the feelings and so on – the role is just slightly different.

'What if I don't want to be a mum?' That might be a question that comes up for some people and my answer to that is simply, 'Well, you don't have to.' I don't believe that every woman needs to become a mother to feel complete. But you do need to be a woman to be a mother. In saying that, I mean that although you need to be a female to actually be a mother, I don't believe that the two must always go together. For example, in a same sex marriage, a male could take on a 'motherly' role without being female in gender. Conversely, a woman needn't feel less than whole if she chooses not to undertake this role in her life. Then there are those woman who will never feel whole until they have children. This is truly something that every individual will need to dig down deep inside to find out whether that's something that they really want to become.

After looking back over this chapter, some things for you to act on and remember are:

1. If you are a new mum, here are some daily affirmations that I would like you to write down somewhere of note … and read out loud every day!

    a. Mums are amazing – I'm amazing

    b. I give my best – and my best is always enough

    c. I am my babies' world – they love me completely, and they never judge

And, if you're not coping, please, please, please don't alienate yourself and don't feel like you have to put on this false show for everybody else that you're coping amazingly. Everybody struggles as a new mum in some way. Everybody.

If people appear as though they're not struggling, perhaps it's because they've got an amazing support network behind them, but if you are having a hard time and you don't feel like you can reach out to your immediate family or your friends, then please, use the services of organisations like Beyond Blue and PANDA. Beyond Blue has a 24-hour helpline which you can call on 1300 22 4636 as well as an online chat and email messaging system. They also have plenty of articles you can research online that may help reassure you that you aren't alone as well as give you some ideas around coping and where to go next. PANDA is also a great organisation with loads of online information that you can easily access such as frequently asked questions, counsellors, and links to further resources. Their helpline number is 1300 726 306.

www.beyondblue.org.au

www.panda.org.au

2. If you're sitting there wondering if you are or have been a good mum to date, and are chastising yourself for your mistakes, please don't. All any good mother can do is her best and that's the most anybody can ever ask for.

If you are raising your children and giving them the best you can give them – you're feeding them the best food that you could feed them, and making sure they go to school, taking them for treatment when they're sick and so on – then you are doing an amazing job. You are doing the best that you can do with the tools that you have at this particular time. Well done!

3. If you know a new mum, just be ears that listen and arms that can pat them on the shoulder and tell them that they are doing great. Give them encouragement, but also let them know that you are there even if they just need 5 minutes for themselves. Just knowing that someone is there and supports and doesn't judge is amazing and can make all the difference when needed.

Osu

Chapter 1 – A New Mum is Born

Notes

Chapter 2

Kids: Kryptonite for Supermums

Just because you can do anything, doesn't mean you can do everything.

– Author unknown

Superman. The man of steel. Virtually untouchable. Bullet proof. Seemingly invincible, except when he encounters that little piece of green rock. But why does that little piece of stone affect him so much? Well, apparently, it's because kryptonite is a stone from the remains of his home planet, Krypton. A piece of his birthplace, a part of himself and where he comes from. It is his one weakness.

I liken that weakness to the feeling of powerlessness our children often give us. Of course, we are the parents and so we do have the control, but this feeling of not having it originates from somewhere deep inside ourselves and is evoked by looking at or listening to that tiny piece of ourselves standing in front of us. It's not a bad place and I believe it almost always comes from a place of love.

When we look at our children, we don't just see them but feel them. I don't believe we are always aware of this and, often, when it does dawn on us we are somewhat taken by surprise. So, when they are there demanding something from us, deep inside we see and feel ourselves wanting it and we want to please them so much that we often cave and provide it, even if it's an unreasonable request.

Or, there are times when we're just flabbergasted by their behaviour – how dare they behave like that and have another tantrum? This horror of ours must come from shame or embarrassment as we look at that bad behaviour and, in some ways, compare this to ourselves. I mean, we wouldn't behave like that, right? So why would they?

Perhaps we just don't really understand what's going on inside of them. Often we just get worn down, feel weak and give in, or perhaps then behave in a manner in which we would not normally.

But it's not just those little green monsters that make us weak and drain our powers. We also have the other kryptonite to fight against, and that is the whole Supermum myth!

To be perfectly honest, I don't even like the term 'Supermum'. Today, I think the term is supposed to describe a woman who is a mother, has a career, always looks and plays the part and seemingly has it all under control. I think, however, this is a little insulting to stay-at-home mums who are actually quite super themselves. They're the ones who always seem to have the house clean and have homemade baked goods, they're the ones that do the crafty ideas with the children, the laundry's always done and these are the ones who are the school volunteers, always helping out where they can. Maybe we just need to get rid of the Supermum myth and stop trying to be that and just be good or a great mum. If we don't dispel this Supermum myth, then we'll always be in the shadow of a fictional superhero and we may never see our own true power and light.

Eliminating the Supermum myth is important because by doing that we can remove some stress in our lives. If we can allow ourselves to stop worrying about attempting to be this Supermum and trying to live up to this unrealistic expectation, then we can start to just be Mum and put away our cape. We can stop feeling bad about having a weakness. I mean, if Superman has one, then surely it's okay if we do!

Letting go of the Supermum idea will help us be happier mums with happier kids. I remember reading that there is no such thing as true multitasking, that you simply cannot apply 100% of your focus or ability to more than one task at a time effectively. Something will suffer. Isn't that what we're trying to do when we want to be Supermum? We're trying to do everything amazingly all at once.

For a time, I found it hard to accept that I was indeed a mum, let alone a super mum. In some ways I felt like having the kids was my kryptonite, like it made me less or weaker than I was. This was especially so for me in my role as a martial arts instructor.

I remember all the times that I was pregnant – 3 times, 27 months of my life – and trying to continue running my martial arts and fitness club – teaching classes and looking after office work. When I first got pregnant, I was afraid that my existing students wouldn't want to train with me because of it. Like suddenly I wasn't capable anymore. I know it's crazy, but it's something that went through my mind. What I thought was even worse, was that when new students would come in and meet me and look and see me pregnant, I thought they would think, 'Oh, she's going to teach me… but she's pregnant.' I don't know why I felt like that, but I did and it was hard. I am so grateful to everybody who supported me and stayed and trained and didn't even bat an eyelid when I was teaching while pregnant. Or, indeed, teaching once I'd had the babies and would whip off to the back room in between classes to breast feed and then come back out, wrap my baby up with a hug-a-bub baby sling and continue yelling and counting and teaching with this baby sleeping on my chest.

I suppose there were people who thought that I was a Supermum, but I was never trying to be. I just wanted to still be able to do everything that I did before and I needed to have my baby there with me to do that.

There was definitely a moment when I realised that it was more than okay. I had one particular member of mine who came in, who was a really strong fighter and wanted to jump into the ring for a fight. At this time, I had a very new baby but I still wanted to go to the tournament to be in his corner. He was my student, my fighter, and I needed to be there. Nobody else could do that job for me. I had to go. I remember sitting in the carpark feeding the baby before I went in, hoping that he would just go to sleep and that I could do what I needed to do on that night.

I did that – fed the baby, put him in my hug-a-bub and entered the venue, feeling a little bit silly, to be honest. I wondered what my fighter – my student – would think. Would he be embarrassed to have a coach on his side who was standing there with a new baby? Fortunately for me, the baby did sleep and slept the whole way through from being out the back doing the fight prep, wrapping hands, putting on the oil, the Vaseline, getting the fighter ready to go into the ring and then walking out to this big, loud venue where people were cheering and I had to coach. When I had to climb up onto the side of the ring and be there – be the representative for my fighter – I felt a little bit embarrassed, but nobody else seemed to even really take notice. In fact, later on, my fighter told me that he was actually really proud to have me in his corner and thought it showed what a strong woman and coach I was. It meant a lot for him to say that to me – probably more than he knew.

In regards to being Supermum, there are days when, in the morning, I simply want things to be able to run smoothly. I just want the kids to be able to get up, get ready and I hope to be able to walk out the door with their hair done, their teeth brushed, their bags packed. I want to have the best possible lunch I can put in their lunchbox to send them off to school with, in the best possible way. And that's a hard job. If I look at my experiences even over the last week, I have definitely not been Supermum.

There have been the times when I've slept in and had to rush, have my shower, then try to get kids out of bed as well because they've slept in and then I'm getting them ready, and this is where it gets hard because it's very easy to then turn to the kids and say, 'Well, you did this to me – you made me late', but, in actual fact, it was my fault.

They're kids, and kids have no concept of time. You can send them upstairs for socks and they come downstairs with a toy and three books. That can be really frustrating and I've lost my cool on more than one occasion, but I can't chastise myself for that, because getting ready in the morning is difficult and I need to accept the fact that kids don't look at it the same way I do and it's rarely going to run smoothly. It's my responsibility to make plans to get up earlier so that I'm not in such a rush, so I don't need to yell, and I don't need to put the pressure on the kids, causing it all to go to pot.

We need to forget about trying to be Supermum. Accept that we won't always accomplish everything on our to-do list … and we don't have to. Sometimes the children simply wear you down and break you and if you can accept that, you don't have to feel like they make you weak. You don't have to feel like you need to blame them for anything and you can get on with being Mum.

Some of you might say, 'The kids always get the better of me.' I guess one way to tackle that is to make some house rules. Write them down and put them on a canvas, in a picture frame, or list them on a chalkboard and hang it up somewhere in the house, like in the kitchen, where everyone is often congregating and it's a visual cue for everybody to see.

If the kids can't read, you could put little pictures or make signs, but this way they're up there for you and the kids and it's a reminder for everybody. Also show if there's disciplinary action that needs to be taken for breaking the rules. It might be a point system or it might be alone time or quiet time or toys removed. It's your choice here, but whatever it is, that choice needs to be made clear to everyone so that when the issue arises or the child acts up in a way that you don't want them to behave, then you can look at your little chart and have an appropriate response. Maybe that's going to help you to deal with misbehaviour a little bit better. The kids won't get the better of you so much or, when they do, you can turn that around.

If you don't manage to be strong and you do lose your cool, then one thing you can do is apologise. There have been many times when I have gotten angry, raised my voice, acted in a way that I feel was perhaps childish and very un-Supermum-like, and I've had to go into my daughter's or sons' room and sit them down and say, 'Listen … Mummy's sorry.' Apologising is never a sign of weakness. When we do that with our children it's actually a big sign of strength and it's teaching them to behave in a manner that you'd want to behave yourself. You are demonstrating how you'd expect them to behave if they were to get angry, hurt or upset with a sibling or a friend or another family member, or someone at school. You're showing them. You're leading by example.

Then you might say, 'But I still want to be a Supermum' and my response to that would be to remember this: Your kids don't want or need a Supermum. They need a mum who loves and cares for them, and is happy and fun to be around. Be that, and that is super enough!

Here, at the end of this chapter, there are a couple of points I'd like to emphasise:

1. Give yourself some credit. Even Superman had his weakness. If you're going to have one, then it might as well be something as wonderful as failing to be a superhero or, at times, feeling like your kids have gotten the better of you. Think of the saying, 'Shoot for the moon and if you miss, you will still land on a star.'

2. Remember that you don't need to save the world. You don't need to be a superhero. The only thing you need to do is provide a loving environment for your kids to grow up in and help them to be healthy and happy. That's all you need to do. And if you can do that, you're super anyway.

Osu

Notes

Chapter 3

Nobody Told Me That

Do the best you can until you know better.
Then when you know better, do better.
– Maya Angelou

Looking back over my time so far as a mother, I realise there are many things that I didn't know because nobody told me. I used to think I wanted to be more than my mum. Not more as a person, but I wanted a license to drive, a career and money to spare and I often fantasised that her life must have been great and easy going as a stay-at-home mum. Of course, she never told me how much hard work it was to raise a child. I now know that it took much of her day to make my breakfast, lunches, make sure I got dressed, do my hair, walk me to school and then go home, only to come back, pick me up and walk me back home again.

Of course, then there was also all the housework in between, dinners, bath time, reading and then settling again for bed.

Yes, unlike my mum, I currently run my own business and I have my driving license and can drive my kids to school and other places that we need to go to, etc., but sometimes now I think all that's done is make my life busier. I travel further and more because I can, but for the short while that I rented a house close enough to walk to school from, I really did enjoy that time. Scooters and bikes, time for chats, fresh air and so on, and I started to wonder if, perhaps, she did in fact do motherhood better than me.

Nobody told me that although at times we criticise our parents, one day it will come back and bite us on the proverbial. So, Mum, I have to admit and say you did a wonderful job, because I think that I turned out pretty okay. When my turn came to be Mummy, I didn't realise there would be days when I would lose my temper so much I'd say things I didn't mean, or harshly discipline my kids and later sit in the shower and cry about it, chastising myself. Maybe that's okay, because at least crying showed that I cared enough to feel bad and wanted to be better at parenting tomorrow.

I don't know if that's what my mum did when she yelled at me. I remember the getting scolded bit well enough. At least, the really bad ones. But she didn't tell me then how it felt on her end. I do know, however, that if my mum were wrong, she would almost always come back later and apologise or explain.

I can distinctly remember being around 14 years old and having my period and hating having to use those gigantic sanitary pads. I honestly felt like I was walking around in a dirty nappy and that everyone could see it. All the books I read and the magazine articles in Dolly and Cleo tried to reassure me that nobody could see it or smell it, which was also my fear, but I didn't believe them. I felt it, it was uncomfortable, and I would dread my period every month.

Chapter 3 – Nobody Told Me That

One day, whilst reading my coveted Dolly mag, I saw an ad for a free trial for mini tampons which explained that anyone could use them and there was a whole article explaining how and why they were a good idea.

All I had to do was fill in and mail off a coupon and they would be delivered in a discreet package. It was a no-brainer to me. I filled in my little coupon and waited in anticipation for my carefree freedom to arrive in the letterbox. I got home from school one day and my special brown paper box was there. I opened it, excited, and then hid the contents in my bottom drawer underneath a stash of clothes.

A little bit later, Mum came in and calmly asked what was in my delivery. Dammit. I thought I'd gotten away unnoticed. Not wanting to lie, I told Mum, and all of a sudden I watched her face change and she got so angry and eventually asked why I wanted them, calling me sneaky, etc. She blurted out something about that meaning that I must've been having sex. I was a bit taken aback and jumped to my own defence, but then we were just yelling and Mum stormed out, slamming the door. I was embarrassed and also so mad. I can't remember what I did, but it probably just entailed me turning up the music on my pink ghetto blaster really loudly and just trying to not go out of my room, in case I ran into my mum. Gosh, what did I do all that time in my room with no computer, no internet, and no mobile phone? Makes me laugh now to think about that.

What I remember the most was Mum coming back later to apologise and explain why she had gotten so mad. I don't need to go into detail about that and I don't remember exactly what she said, but I think it was something about meaning I was growing up and her fears were coming up … but the gist here is that she came and apologised. Though I didn't realise it then, by her doing this, she was telling me how to act and parent, and showing me that apologising wasn't a sign of weakness; I just didn't know how to listen. And the answer to your question is no, I wasn't (if that's what you were thinking).

I'm pretty sure that, if I sit back and look, there were plenty of times when I drove my mum bonkers, but it felt like nobody – my mum or anyone else – had told me that my own kids would do the same to me. That they would turn my life upside down, inside and out and I wouldn't even notice it when it happened … and even if I did, I'd be powerless to stop it. I didn't realise that once I had children of my own, every time I made a decision about anything from here on in, I would automatically consider them first and I would feel like at times my life wasn't even my own anymore and that I wasn't a priority to myself. Even now, when I need a haircut do you think I can, for the life of me, find the time to get one? Plus, I simply can't justify spending the money right now when my son needs a new mattress and my daughter has school camp, amongst the many other things on the to-do list. Before I had kids, when other mums would talk about things like that, I thought they were crazy. I mean, wouldn't you look after yourself first, right?

We'll touch on that more a bit later, but who knew, hey, that I would turn out to be exactly like all the other 'crazy' mums!

Nobody told me that after I gave birth my large belly wouldn't just disappear. That I'd be left with this saggy, squishy, messy thing that I would need to squeeze every morning into a huge piece of elastic to hold it all together while it reduced, ever painfully, as my uterus shrank back to its original size with each breastfeed. That I would wear that very unsexy piece of equipment and I'd love it.

Nobody told me that I'd cry with each feed in the early days and sit at home and wonder if I'd ever be able to leave my baby's side. Then, when I'd stop crying, I would sit and feel torn by wanting to just be there for my new baby, but also wanting to be able to do everything I used to do … and then I'd worry about that, and later, when I was exhausted enough, I just fell asleep.

Nobody warned me that each night when my baby would cry, I would think, 'Please, please, just bloody go back to sleep.' Then, when they did, I'd be up every 15 minutes to check if they were still breathing.

Nobody told me that I would feel like I didn't fit in with the other mums at school and kinder and that I'd have a hard time and feel awkward at kids' parties. I didn't feel the same as them as I really thought I should be all about baby – as it seemed they were – and not back at work and teaching and training. I didn't think I had anything to talk with them about, and I often felt kind of separate. I know we did have things in common, but I felt it was only the bad stuff and I didn't want my interactions with others to always be about going over my gripes and moans and hard times.

Sometimes I just felt that I was the only one struggling and trying to juggle everything and they were doing just fine. I hated having to turn down invitations to lunch or coffee and feeling like the outcast as I was always saying, 'No, I have to train' or 'I have to teach' or 'I have the kids'. 'Sorry, I can't' became an almost auto reply text message.

Nobody told me that some days I'd be flying by the seat of my pants and pretty much winging it – that I wouldn't have all the answers and there would be times when I would have to go with my gut instinct and hope that it all turned out okay. For example, when my babies cried, I always picked them up and settled them. I believed co-sleeping was safe and the best option for us both, even though I had people telling me negative things about it. Sometimes it was 'go with my gut on this' or no sleep for either of us. Later … which kinder to send the kids to, and should I go back to work and put baby in childcare or not? (I'm actually wondering now if most of us are winging it and we just don't let on.)

I also never even considered the fact that one day I might be a single parent and I don't think any of us saw that coming. Nobody told me that parenting on your own is hard – that you don't have that other mediator there to step in when it all gets too much. You don't have someone else to play the good cop or bad cop, and vice versa. I have learned so much already but as my children grow I know that there are so many new problems, experiences, milestones and celebrations to come. Looking forward, I have no doubt that there is still very much more that I don't know.

I'm reminded now of this quote by Donald Rumsfeld: 'There are known knowns; there are things we know we know. But we also know there are known unknowns. That is to say, we know there are some things we do not know. But there are also unknown unknowns – the ones we don't know we don't know.'

In the case of parenting, I'm starting to think that maybe we just aren't supposed to know everything beforehand. After all, would you really have listened? Had someone told you everything upfront, would it have actually made a difference to the way that you've parented so far? Would you have honestly still decided to become a parent? In many ways, I'm glad I got to discover the challenges in motherhood myself and make up my own mind about them. I'm also now beginning to wonder if, like childbirth, the intensity of the pain wears off and although you don't essentially forget, these negative things lose their impact over time. Maybe that's just not the stuff that others remember the most.

Perhaps the struggles and the problems aren't the things

which stand out in a parent's mind afterwards, and this is why I wasn't forewarned about all the bad stuff to come. If it's true that love conquers all, it would make sense then that the little wins along the way – the cuddles and the kisses and the first footsteps and the tiny miracles and the giggling fits – shine much more light onto us than the bad times cast shadows over us. The good always triumphs over evil and in the end love is all we need.

Indeed, it's true that even if someone had told me that one day I would be crying due to exhaustion as a new mother, and one first little smile would light up my being and give me the strength to soldier through the whole day on 3 hours' sleep and constant breast feeding, I would not have believed them.

And if someone had told me that there would come a time when I'd be in the bathroom, clapping my hands and singing a celebration song and doing a victory dance about a poo in the potty, that I would not have believed them, either. If my mum had said that on the days when my kids would be so difficult as to drive me to distraction and almost make me lose my mind, that at night when I put them to bed and they look like sleeping angels, that when I kiss their foreheads as they sleep, that I would get a wave of love and peace wash over me and the bad day would flow back into the ocean of memories, I wouldn't have listened to her either. Or maybe I would have listened, but not quite understood.

I believe that knowing information in advance can, of course, help you prepare, but only to a point. Perhaps it is, indeed, part of our journey as mothers and as parents not to know. That we, too, grow by walking the path, facing the obstacles together with our children, going through the struggles and celebrating achievements and relishing the times that we manage to get things right.

What is right for one mother is not necessarily right for others and, as mothers, we pass on our own experiences – both good and bad – to our children and our children are constantly providing us with new lessons, new feedback, in order for us to pass it back onto them in one way or another. What fun would life be if we knew what was just around the corner, anyway? And even if we did know, it would be useless as we can only ever be and act in the now, in the present moment.

One key point to take away from this chapter is:

Don't be afraid of unknowns. You don't need to know everything. Just stay in the moment. You only need to know that you are doing the best you can with everything you have right now, and that is enough.

Osu

Chapter 3 – Nobody Told Me That

Notes

Lover

I was She

Who was that wicked girl last night?
And wherehence did she go?
There are traces of her here still now
Upon my sheets and smudged across my pillow.

Flashes of her dancing, laughing loudly,
Half-remembered dreams run through my head.
She tricked me, teased me, lured him here
Into my home, into my bed.

Only walls can tell what happened then
Or explain the mess been made.
I have questions but no answers;
She is gone – and yet, he stayed.

And then, slowly, as we start to rouse
From our un-resting drunken slumber,
Realisation that she is me creeps in,
Bursting the foggy spell that I was under.

Here it lies, the stripped-off evidence
I see strewn across the floor.
My heart sinks; another piece of me departs
Along with him … out through my door

Chapter 4

Where Did My Sexy Go?

Darling, I never step on the scale, because the scale doesn't measure sexy.
– Bella Dolce

In 2011, in the UK, a magazine called A Beautiful Mummy took a poll of 3000 women and found that it takes, on average, 18 months for a mother to feel attractive and like a woman again after giving birth. That's 547 days. 547 days of feeling unattractive and not yourself – and that's just an average. For many women, it is much longer. Then couple that with women who get pregnant again just outside of or near to that time and the effect is compounded. That's years of not feeling like the woman you were before.

As I have mentioned previously, I had to wear a supportive garment after birth just to hold my jiggly tummy in. None of my clothes fit. My 'me' clothes that I wore before pregnancy were too small and my pregnancy clothes were too big. I pretty much lived in stretchy gym gear … and it's funny, though, because it's pretty much all I wear now and I don't care. But it was the lack of choice that counted. Not having the option to be able to wear whatever I wanted, when I couldn't wear anything else, I felt restricted because I couldn't simply put on a nice dress if I was going out, or my favourite pair of jeans.

There may be some of you who didn't feel this way. You might have been able to pop back on your clothes or felt comfy in early pregnancy gear, but lots of us don't. The other thing that can happen after childbirth is not being able to see yourself as a woman any more – seeing yourself as just you. The person who you were before. Your body can sometimes feel like a vessel. You have now given birth and your body has adjusted to allow for that miracle to be conceived, nourished, constructed and born, and now it must also go through a process of adjusting to feed your baby and set off a series of chemical reactions that physically set out to return your body to its pre-pregnancy state.

Breast milk is formed and this process triggers uterine contractions that help to shrink the expanded uterus. This can be mildly to extremely painful. Breast-feeding, we think, looks completely easy and should be second nature, right? My first child had no trouble feeding, but for the small-chested person that I am, when my milk came in I had these massive jugs that would wake me up in the middle of the night, swollen and hard and leaking all over the bed and I had to sit in the bathroom, plugged up to a breast pump like a cow on a dairy farm so that I didn't have to wake my finally sleeping daughter to relieve the pressure and pain.

In the first few days, my nipples also cracked and were so painful that when my daughter cried to be fed I would panic and cry myself as I knew how much it was going to hurt, how much pain I was going to be in. It felt like razor blades coming out of me.

Chapter 4 – Where Did My Sexy Go?

I hated the fact that I didn't want to feed her and that I knew I had to. At one point, I remember walking around the house topless as any clothing touching my chest hurt too much. Nice, right? Not. It's funny now, of course, and I can laugh, but at the time I felt anything but good about my body and myself. I felt like a cow, as though I should change my name to Daisy or Dairy or something.

I was also confused a little bit about who I was. I was now a mother and not just me. Part of me thought I would now be viewed differently by my friends, peers and partner as well. After all, when are mums still sexy, or are they even allowed to be? Of course, I know now that they are, but with all those emotions and hormones swimming around in my head, rational thoughts were not always at the forefront of my thinking in those early days. Not being able to wear your clothes again, or just being unhappy with what you see in the mirror after child birth can spell trouble in regards to feeling sexy and womanly. This can make us less able to allow ourselves to be a lover – to be open and able to be an affectionate and giving partner in a relationship. I will add that this doesn't only apply to mothers. Many women are not happy with their physical appearance prior to childbirth, either.

This, I'm sure, is no surprise to you. You only have to be in a conversation with a group of women when the topic of figures or sports or gym comes up to know this. Even amongst young women. This part of our makeup permeates way deeper into our lives than we may even give credit to or know. Couple this, then, with the after-effects of childbirth, and you are in for a double whammy!

When I say, 'Where did my sexy go?' I say sexy but what I really mean is confidence. You know, confidence is sexy and confidence is always attractive. And it's important for us to feel confident and attractive, because if we have this, then it's likely that we're more able to go out and get the things that we want in life and to have more success simply because we're driven and not held back by a lack of confidence. If we have this feeling of sexiness and confidence, we're going to allow ourselves to have more fulfilling relationships because we won't be holding ourselves back in fear or prevent ourselves from getting closer with our chosen partner.

Feeling attractive and loveable and sexual is a very, very real need for us emotionally and this is not something that we should deny ourselves. If we don't find our sexy – if we don't find our confidence – then we are going to miss out on these things that we could have gotten if we didn't hold ourselves back. We're going to spend our time feeling less than we should and we will suffer emotionally because of it and we might not find love. As a single mother, we might not find love at all, or we might just find a type of love that we don't want to have, and go after people whom we don't really want to be with simply because we don't have the confidence or belief in ourselves to go out and find the ones we do want.

As a mother in a relationship, we may miss out on the deep and fulfilling partnership that we could have if we were truly able to offer ourselves over to our partner in all the ways that we should. Having that confidence in our appearance and our attractiveness to our partners makes us feel secure. When we feel secure in our relationships, there is less tension and more rewarding communication and interaction between lovers.

Feeling attractive and wanted as a mate is something that we all strive for. Embedded deep into our psyche is our need to have a loving partner. There's no doubt that body image plays a part in that, and I'm not going to say that it shouldn't because that would be a waste of time. It always will. However, I really do believe that after the initial meeting where that first impression counts so much, including the visual makeup of the people involved, the focus will shift towards emotions brought up by behaviours. In a very simplistic look on behaviours, we know that the way we act has much to do with our values and how we see ourselves. Feeling good about ourselves is imperative if we want to act in a manner that will attract the person that we want to have in our lives, or maintain an existing relationship or marriage.

On the other hand, part of feeling good may be remembering that it's not only about looks. Men do find a certain attractiveness in watching a mother nurture a child. Perhaps, in part, it reminds them of their love for their own mother. It has been said, 'Being sexy isn't about the size you are or how pretty you are; it's about making a man feel like a man' (Author unknown).

You know, another way to find your sexy if you feel like you've lost it is to find out what makes you specifically feel sexy … and this is different for everyone. For me, feeling fit and strong and powerful makes me feel capable, and that makes me feel sexy. It could be something different for you. You might look at what you find sexy in other women – when you're watching a movie and a particular movie star appeals to you because you think they're sexy, or you notice somebody in a magazine, or perhaps someone you know in your everyday life – and you look at them and you go, 'Wow, they're really sexy.' Ask yourself what the characteristics of that person are that makes them sexy, and that's going to tell you what you think is sexy, and so that's what you need to try and look for and find within yourself.

The other thing is to stop being your own worst critic. For example, if someone tells you that they think you are beautiful, you should believe them. And if you can't believe them, then believe that they believe, and just believe in the possibility that maybe you are.

You might be sitting there thinking, 'But I just don't feel sexy', and I implore you to find out why so you can address this. As I said before, look at it and find out what you think is sexy and why you feel that you're not. If it's a lack of fitness, go and join a gym. If it's guilt about being sexy – maybe you feel like you shouldn't be sexy for some reason – then you need to let that go. If you think, 'I don't want to feel sexy because my partner doesn't like it', then I'd say that's pretty dangerous ground and you need to open some channels of communication with your partner, because perhaps this is more about their insecurities and has nothing to do with you. It's an indication of their own lack of self-confidence and, in some ways, this can be a very controlling thing, so please, very carefully watch if they're the words that you're speaking right now. A loving partner who is confident with themselves will want you to feel sexy. They will want you to feel good about yourself, and they will want their relationship enhanced.

You might be feeling guilty because you're a mum and feel that you shouldn't be a sexy, sexual being anymore. I'm going to say, 'You know what? No. You owe it to your kids.' Remember that it's really important to show your kids your confidence, because how they see you will shape who they become and what sort of relationships they choose in the future. Jump online or get a book on psychology and look up a Freudian term called 'repetition compulsion'. This is a neurotic defence mechanism and it basically works by us trying to rewrite history. It's typical in our intimate relationships where we look to recreate the relationship that we had with a parent, or recreate the relationship our parents had with each other. Even though sometimes we may not even want that, we look for it in such a way that it's almost like we're forcing ourselves to relive these relationships until we learn the lessons we need to from them. For example, if a parent we identified with had been in a controlling relationship, we might choose controlling partners until we reach a point in our lives where we see this occurring and do something to change that.

You can look into this more if you are interested. It's so important for you to find your sexy and your confidence and create loving relationships, because your kids are watching. You owe it to them to be sexy and to allow yourself to be a lover, because you're teaching them through the way you're behaving in your relationships.

At the end of this chapter, I want you to remember a couple of important things:

1. You need to see yourself as beautiful. The power of suggestion is mighty – to yourself and to those around you. Remember that we teach people how to treat us by how we talk about and treat ourselves, so please instruct people the right way.

2. Please remember that looks aren't everything, but do whatever you need to do, to 'get your sexy back'. Learn dancing, get fit and strong, learn a sexy, exotic new language, buy new clothes, get a haircut, and so on. But the number one thing is, don't leave it too late. Women are the masters in the art of reinventing themselves after a breakup. Don't wait until you're in a position where you need to rescue your life before you do it. As they say, a stitch in time saves nine. Please … I implore you, go out and get your sexy back.

Osu

Notes

Chapter 5

It's Not Me, It's Them

> Every time I thought I was being rejected from something good, I was actually being redirected to something better.
> **– Dr Steve Maraboli**

I wish I could go back and tell my 15-year-old self not to worry about relationships – that it didn't matter who didn't find me attractive, that someone didn't want to be my boyfriend, because one day the right one would. When I was growing up, the first few times a boyfriend broke up with me, it felt like my world was ending. I couldn't imagine getting through the rest of the school day or night, let alone surviving every day without them.

I felt sick inside and as though my inner walls came crashing down. Everybody handles this differently. I used to sit in my room and cry and write sad poetry. It helped to write and to get it off my chest, but it also enabled me, at times, to stay in that negative and sad frame of mind and obsess about and overanalyse my feelings. Sometimes analysing feelings is good, but only if you're able to step back and be constructive about them, and not be enveloped by them.

I was always embarrassed to show emotion around my family and sometimes my friends, and even at this point in my life at 40 years old I still am, to some extent. Back then, though, I had nobody older or more experienced whom I felt that I could bounce this stuff off. I wondered why I wasn't good enough and it ate at my insecurities. Was I not pretty enough? Were my boobs too small? Were my legs too skinny? Was I too short? Too loud? Or were my clothes not cool enough? Was it because I couldn't water ski or dance right? Or was my family not rich enough and I lived in the wrong suburb? I didn't know then that sometimes you can have it all and be what you think is great, but the object of your affection still won't feel the same.

That's because another person's lack of interest in you is about them and not you. It's important for us to try to understand and deal with rejection in more positive ways, by replacing these illogical ideas with more logical ones. We need to stop the spiral of feeling rejection and then continuously being rejected. The benefit of learning to deal with this better is that it allows for a more detached perspective. We are able to separate our feelings from our thinking, thus having a more analytical way of looking at things instead of reacting purely emotionally. It also allows us to get over things and move forward quicker instead of staying and wondering why certain things happen.

There's a psychological healing technique founded by Albert Ellis called Rational Emotive Behavioural Therapy, or REBT. REBT proposes that the reason that you felt what you felt has to do with your pre-existing and underlying beliefs and philosophies about getting the approval, companionship, support, intimacy, etc., of another. Using this therapy, patients are asked to look at what they say to themselves about rejection and how to consider more logical, beneficial and truthful alternatives to try and create healthier emotional and behavioural responses. With regards to rejection in terms of finding a lover or partner, this type of thinking is highly beneficial. It can also be of use when dealing with rejection within an existing partnership.

If we don't learn to deal with rejection in a healthy way, it eats at our self-esteem and we live in fear of it and it often prevents a happy future by restricting our boundaries or even our opportunity to find love or ability to feel like we can be loved.

Revisit the quote at the beginning of this chapter. That's a healthy way of looking at things. Hard to do in that particular moment, but if you can sit back and say, 'At this point in time I'm being told no, but that's because something better is around the corner', it will be easier to accept. As I said, easy to say, hard to do, but worth trying.

When I propose that it's not you, it's them, I'm not suggesting to always cast blame. I am saying that accepting responsibility is the only way we can stay in power and it's the only way we can change. When it comes to romance, or even other areas where we can be rejected, thinking it's your fault or something is wrong with you and you aren't perfect for anyone, is just not true.

If I look back at my last relationship, my relationship of 11 years with the father of my children, and I analyse (or overanalyse) that, I could say that the fact that I lived in anxiety and fear for a very long time was all my fault – that I was somehow weak or not good enough and attribute all the failure to a fault in me – but, really, some of those issues, some of that anxiety and some of that fear came from his behaviour as well.

It wasn't that I was weak, or I wasn't good enough. Some of it was caused by actions that he took, which fuelled my reactions and the subsequent thought processes within me. Part of me wishes that I could've been able to deal with those things better at the time, but it's not until now and being able to step back, separating myself emotionally from the issues, that I can look at it and be a little bit more analytical about it and break things down and see it from a different perspective.

Since I separated, there have been other attempted relationships. One particular person whom I started to see was younger than myself and didn't have children. Although I thought we were a great match and we spent time together and it was always great and I felt a really deep connection with this person, he didn't want a relationship with me – not a long-term one, anyway – and initially I started to do the thing I had done in the past. I asked myself the same old questions: Did that mean that I wasn't good enough? Was I not pretty enough? The same things … it's these things that keep coming up consistently, so I decided to just ask the question, for once.

I asked him simply, 'Why? Why not me?' And the answers came back and, fortunately for me, he was always honest and plainly stated that he wanted someone around his age, someone without kids. He wasn't ready to take on children now although he did want to have children of his own but not until sometime in the future. What that says is that it wasn't necessarily about me, but it was about my predicament. It wasn't that I wasn't good enough, but it was just not the right situation or the right time in both our lives.

I realised soon after that I had begun to choose people who I knew wouldn't stay. I was picking partners who weren't suitable for a long-term relationship. I did that subconsciously because although I did want them to stay, I knew that they wouldn't and by knowing this, part of me thought that I was not setting myself up for disappointment. In the end I was, and it's easy to step back now and say, 'Well, that was a bit silly – I shouldn't have done that', but at the time I didn't realise what I was doing. I couldn't be angry at the fact that they weren't going to stay, because that's the whole reason I chose them in the first place.

Some of you might ask, 'But if there isn't anything wrong with me, why doesn't this person want to be with me?' I can only reply by saying to remember that everybody is moving through life and going through different experiences, and when it comes to relationships and friendships they are part of the learning we do to find out where we fit in life and who we are. I guess it may be that a particular person has a lesson meant for you, and once you learn it perhaps it is time for them to part ways with you as you're ready for your next lesson or your time with them is just finished. Some people are there, I think, for the short-term and others for much, much longer.

If you meet a person whom you feel is your ideal mate, but they don't feel the same way about you, it can be hard to not take that personally. The best way to handle this situation again, I think, is communication. Ask why, like I did, and then listen to the answer and don't place your own pre-existing beliefs on it. There will indeed be times when you aren't the sort of person that another one is attracted to, but you shouldn't get upset, though, because if you stop and think about it, there are plenty of others out there who are great people, but you aren't attracted or interested in them. So does that mean that there is something wrong with them? No? It's just that you aren't a match and that's okay.

Inside of an existing relationship, there may be times when an idea you have put forward is rejected by your partner. It may be a suggestion for a holiday destination, a change of residence, or even a request against an unwanted physical advance. When a partner doesn't agree with us and rejects our ideas it can make us believe that we aren't an equal in the relationship. An example may be that the mother is not working, and stays at home and looks after the kids. Due to this, the father is the sole income earner for the family. The mother may suggest that the kids need new beds, and the father could turn around and say no and iterate that he has the final say as it's 'his' money. This situation could escalate quickly if not resolved. That type of dismissal may make the mother feel as though she is less than capable of making a financial decision, make her feel unequal, un-needed, and could severely impact her sense of pride and self-worth. This, in turn, would make her turn away from her partner, and the relationship would start a decline in all other areas. Again, with communication, it may come to light that the father's negative comments stemmed from his frustration at feeling like he has all the responsibility financially, and it may simply be stress that caused him to react in this way. So, we see here another example of the person who is being rejected not being the total cause of this. Communication, once more, is key.

Another thing that's also worth considering is that when we are rejected, we're told, 'No, you can't have what you want'. It could be employment, a specific outfit at a store or a date with a person whom we like, or an ongoing relationship, but it's more about how we feel about ourselves than what others are saying or denying us that is affecting us negatively. Go back and revisit the REBT system that we talked about earlier.

You might be thinking, 'Oh, but it has to be about me. It can't be all about them … it's all about me!' If you're really thinking that this is so, then maybe it's time to sit down and analyse what it actually is and see if that is something you want to – and can –actually change.

Just remember this wonderful quote from Dita Von Teese: 'You can be the ripest, juiciest peach in the world and there's still going to be someone who hates peaches.' It's a good quote and allows us to have a bit of humour in a situation, which I think is also important.

At the end of this chapter there are some things that I'd like you to remember:

1. Handling rejection well is not for the other person's benefit. It's not about how we want others to perceive us, but more about protecting ourselves and keeping a healthy, emotional perspective. This is for us now and to carry on into the future.

2. Be mindful. Note your reactions to things – even the little things. E.g. You asked someone out for dinner and they said no? You got upset and noted that it was because you felt embarrassed instead of unworthy. Or, you reached out to hold your partner's hand and they pulled away. You got angry because you felt they didn't want to be intimate with you, and you thought it was because you weren't attractive enough. If you can start to look at the whys then you can start a process of analysing your responses a little bit better.

3. Get a pen and paper and purge. Let go of any thoughts you have about yourself that keep on bringing up feelings of rejection. If you write down all those feelings and you're horrified at what comes out, then burn that list if you want as maybe that's another way to let go of it. Or you can just keep notes – keep a diary, an old fashioned diary. Your notes are a great way to write down your responses to things at the end of the day and monitor it. It helps to keep you accountable and if you see things written down on paper it's going to give you an opportunity to change them, because they're there in front of you.

Remember this final thing: you cannot control outcomes. The one thing that you can control is your response.

Osu

Chapter 5 – It's Not Me, It's Them

Notes

Chapter 6

Separation Anxiety

Only in the agony of parting do we look into the depths of love.
— George Eliot

When couples get together, the phrase used is that 'two become one', so it felt for me like one became a half as I separated from my long-term partner. It was scary to think that I was now going to be alone and now going to be a half. You cannot, however, be a half.

I guess the failing of the relationship was a slow process but the actual separation happened quickly. I remember watching the moving van drive away. I felt sick. My kids were watching and I tried not to show them how upset I was. I went into my room and cried … .and then emerged as what I thought was respectable. I had no real answers to their questions. We had talked about it in the weeks leading up to that day with them, but they were young and didn't really understand things until they actually happened.

There were moments when I wanted to stop him from packing the van. To just say, 'Put it all back into the house and stay … We can work this out …' but deep inside I knew we had tried and it was time. There was so much pain there – so many hurtful things said, so many questions – and we had been going around in the same circles for years. Too long. And, though I will admit there were parts of me which, at that point, were glad to see him leave, there were also parts that were being ripped into pieces and the very fabric of my reality was disintegrating before my eyes. What would I do? How would I manage? Who was I now? It took so long to accept, and even longer to move past it. Sometimes I still feel like I'm just emerging from the fog now. There is still some baggage from that time … but I've come to accept that is what life's about. Accumulating experiences and learning lessons, and some of that involves pain.

How do we even begin to accept the fact that we are now separated? Accepting that it's happened is essential to allow forward motion. If we continue to sit with our pain or deny the fact that a separation has happened, it's going to hold us in the present moment and we'll be stuck in the position that we're in.

Trying to look for positives is one way to help yourself accept this new position in life. Some things to look forward to may be alone time or to be just you again. Perhaps another positive in separation is that you'll now have the opportunity to learn. Things are not going to stay the same. Things will change and through that change there will be growth.

There's also a chance for you now for new and a greater love and it may be soon or it may be a long time away, but there is now an opportunity that wasn't there before. The

Chapter 6 – Separation Anxiety

very fact that you've separated from your partner means that something wasn't quite right and it doesn't matter who was wrong or who was right – all that needs to be put aside now – the separation has occurred. Something was wrong and now you have a chance to make something else right.

The other thing is that your kids get a second home. Mine love the fact that they now have two houses, two bedrooms, two Easters, two Christmases, two places to get away to. When they're angry at me they can always remember they can go to their dad's house. That can be positive for the kids.

According to the Australian Bureau of Statistics, one in three marriages ends in divorce. I wasn't married, but I was in a long-term relationship, so I was not alone. Sometimes in that situation, you feel like you're the only one who's being separated, but you aren't on your own. There are many other people in the same predicament, so there is plenty of opportunity to speak to others who've been through the same thing.

If you don't start to look for positives – if you don't believe that you can grow and learn; if you don't see the opportunity for love – then you can continue to live in guilt, maybe, and shame or fear about the future. The future is something that you cannot predict and if you continue to sit there in fear about a future that you can't predict, it will impact your present and then, obviously, your future success. It's important that you look at separation from a different perspective. As separation is considered quite negative and we may be feeling quite negative, try to step back. Try to look at your situation as an outsider looking in.

Psychologically, separation anxiety is defined as 'a developmental stage where a child or infant experiences excessive anxiety when removed or separated from the primary caregiver (usually the mother)' (MedicineNet.com). But separation or coming away from the security and care and the environment of a place and person that you've been used to for years, or even decades, is scary for adults too. Even the word 'separation' sounds bad. It brings up pictures of coming apart, of being detached, breaking and other divisive images.

Remind yourself that you were one before. You're allowed to be scared, but do not be consumed by your fear. We can acknowledge that we are afraid of something without it controlling us completely. Look for opportunities. You could be you or, even better, you could reinvent yourself and become a new you. There are opportunities to do that now. You don't have to justify yourself to a partner. You may have to remind yourself that you still have to be a mum, but you can be a new you, a new woman.

Even if you know that the breakup is better long-term, there will sometimes still be moments when you feel pulled backwards. You'll question whether this is the right path, even if you were the one who made the decision. Sometimes you need to sit with those feelings and be really honest with yourself and remind yourself that there's a reason why that separation happened. Or maybe you need to consider whether there's an opportunity for going back. Is that something you both want to do? Have you talked about it or considered professional help such as counselling? For me, I went through all those moments, multiple times. There were times when it felt like a roller coaster and we did try counselling. I must admit that I didn't put in my best effort, because I felt like the session, for us, was about me being taken to account so that I could be shown how I was in the wrong. That may or may not have been the case, but that's how it felt to me in my heart. But I did try and if you need to have counselling in order to be able to sit more comfortably with the separation, then it's something that you need to consider.

It's also worthwhile to change your words. For example, when the separation happens and you're meeting people and someone asks, 'What's happened?, or 'Are you still with your partner?', or when it comes up in conversation, instead of saying, 'No, I'm separated', if that's something you haven't dealt with yet then perhaps you could turn around and say, 'Oh, we've both decided to move forward.' There are other expressions that you could use, so choose one that feels and sits right with you and doesn't make you feel terrible when you say it.

What if you can't see an advantage to separating? What if you're looking and you can't see the advantage at all? All I can say is that sometimes it's difficult to see and sometimes we don't want to see. But it's worthwhile, at least, to try to step back and look again because, as far as I can tell, there is always a positive side to everything. As I mentioned before, it's not always easy to see when we're caught up in emotions, especially fear or love, and if we're not the one who made the choice for the separation to occur. If we were the ones separated from, then it can be even harder to step back and see the advantages or the positives. But is that true? Is there really no silver lining? Or do we just not want to see, because we still feel like we need to be with this person and thus refuse to look at the positives or even admit that there are any?

Just stand aside and give yourself some time and do be gentle with yourself, but look for positives. Sometimes in life, when we're not looking we don't find them. Let's say, for example, you wake up in the morning and accidentally turn your alarm off instead of pressing snooze. Then you wake up in a shock as you know you're late. You are flustered and have already told yourself this day is going badly. Then you stub your toe on the bath as you rush to get in the shower. After sprinting your way through your bathroom routine, you almost trip on your way downstairs to the kitchen, only to find out the kids have made a mess making their own breakfast and have put all the bad stuff into their lunchboxes. You yell at the kids about the mess and the lunchboxes, and how they just ruined your morning and made you even more late, and mutter out loud that this is all due to your alarm not working properly. So … you are now focused on all the negatives. If you don't start to turn this day around in a hurry, the traffic is about to get really bad … you'll be late to school … and then work … you'll be repeating this story out loud to your co-workers soon … and then your computer will crash … Do you see the negative pattern?

Instead, when you woke up and realised you were late, you could have thought, 'Oh, I must have needed that sleep in. I'd better make a move quickly.' When you noticed your kids had seen you were late and tried to help, you could have thanked them for their best effort as they did make an attempt to assist you, and let go of the mess and the bad lunchbox and been happy they saved you 10 or so minutes. Look for positives amidst the chaos and the negatives. Seek and you shall find.

You might say, 'Oh, I just can't see how I will survive.' Sometimes it can feel like that and you can be overwhelmed, but stay strong. It sounds old and it sounds daggy, but everything will be okay in the end – it always is. We can say this from hindsight. If you look back through your past at things that didn't work out – your first boyfriend, your first major love, your first job – and you thought your world was crumbling and ending, looking back now, though, you're probably relieved, in some respects, that those particular relationships or arrangements or things ended and something better came along afterwards. Or maybe something worse and then something better, but either way you got through it. Stay strong; you will survive.

One thing that can assist with survival is to seek help, whether that's from a friend or a professional, and make plans. If you're worried about surviving financially, there are always things that you can put in place. For example, you could speak to your bank if you have been having trouble paying a credit card debt and suddenly find yourself unable to pay. You can have the interest frozen and a rescue payment plan arranged and may also be able to take out a line of credit to help with relocating costs, etc. They often know more about what is possible to help you than you do. It's their business to know. You could also seek other financial services such as 'My Budget' or research other companies that can help you if you feel overwhelmed.

You may also be able to speak to schools and implement payment plans for fees, and you may now also be eligible for financial assistance from the government to help with school and kinder fees. Perhaps you need to make a new workplace agreement around your available hours. You may now need to leave work earlier to collect kids from school, and so could cut your lunch break short to give you an earlier knock-off time. You won't know what can be organised to help you until you have these conversations, so don't feel like there is no way out and get worked up about it until you know for sure. It's amazing what we can make up in our own head! Not speaking to people makes everything worse, because you don't know what you don't know.

I encourage you to sit down and make plans regarding what you're going to do next. If you did manage to finally see some advantages in this new situation, because you've got some more free time or had some great advice, then start putting together ideas! What are you going to do to capitalise on in this new beginning?

Listing these ideas will start to become your guide – your instructional manual, or map if you will – to show how you're going to move forward.

As I look back on my experience of separation, here is the best advice I can give:

1. Talk, talk, and talk. Talk to a friend or, as I mentioned before, pay a professional. If you've got preconceived ideas about counsellors or psychologists or people in paid professions, then speak to a friend first or ask around. Often other people have used counsellors or someone before and can recommend one to you, and the very fact that you know someone who has seen one may not make you feel so funny about using that as an option.

2. Another great therapy is cuddling your kids often. Do it whenever you get the chance. Don't hibernate in your fears and your devastation, because they can see and they can feel through you. Children have an uncanny knack of looking right through us and absorbing the energies around them. If they can see you are in pain and suffering but won't let on, they will feel helpless about it or even feel like you are pushing them aside due to blame. Plus, cuddles are an awesome way to make yourself feel better. Cuddle a friend if you don't have your children with you. Cuddling your friends is a great way of reminding yourself that you aren't alone, so even though the separation has happened between you and a loved one, having somebody else there for a cuddle is great. Do it more often.

3. Take the opportunity to look within yourself and look to what you think love is and to realise that now there is a greater opportunity to find something better perhaps than you had before.

4. Remember the whys. I want you to remember the whys. Remembering why something happened helps to ground you so you're not left feeling lost, like you don't understand how come something happened. And if it's not of comfort to you to remember the whys, at least it will, if anything, be a lesson and something that you know not to repeat.

Osu

Notes

Woman

The Mighty Queen

Universe, you win this time;
Concede defeat I will.
But I won't stop until I'm dead
And/or my blood is still.

Another cut and so I bleed,
But stone I am not yet.
Armour on and sword in hand,
My battle cry is all you'll get.

Come one, come all, but none shall pass;
I've dug my trenches deep.
I stand atop of every wall
And now I shall not sleep.

My victory assured, and tales
Of legend you shall sing:
Of how an army could not conquer
This mere queen without a king.

Chapter 7

I Am Woman

> I am woman, hear me roar.
> **– Helen Reddy**

My passion is to empower women to embrace themselves through setting healthy goals and unleashing their inner potential. I hope and believe that I can do this through the vehicle of martial arts and fitness and by conveying what I've learned so far on my own journey.

Throughout this book, I have spoken about the importance of feeling good about yourself and your body and why, as a woman and a mother, it can sometimes be challenging to do that. So many women whom I have dealt with through my own training, my classes and my personal training clients are worried about their body not being perfect. Having previously ascertained that there is no such thing as complete perfection, it stands to reason, then, that the perfect body doesn't exist, either.

I dislike the expression, 'He/she has a "good" body'. Usually when someone says this, they're talking about the way a body looks – its visual appeal. I don't want to hear that phrase anymore. An aesthetically pleasing body, and this is different for everyone, is not necessarily a good one. A good body is a strong body. A good body is a fit body. A good body is a limber body.

A good body you can trust to get you from A to B in one piece and unharmed. A good body is healthy and breaks down only when you neglect it. A good body is useful and moves with purpose. A good body perseveres under pressure. A good body is the house of your heart and soul. Clean the windows and let everyone see how beautiful you are inside.

Personally, I want women to be strong. I really want you to get out there and find your strength and let that empower you in every facet of yourself. I believe that our physical, mental and spiritual health are connected. This cannot be denied. We all know that mental health issues manifest in physical symptoms and sometimes these are as serious as skin conditions (chronic ones), cancer and even heart attack and death.

Do not ever think that creating a strong and healthy body won't contribute in some way to a strong and healthy mind. I honestly know that it can. You might laugh, but during my first childbirth, I remember thinking, 'It's okay – this is just like a karate grading. It's going to be long and painful and difficult, but I can do it.' I just wanted to know where I was up to in the process and it was like, 'Oh, okay, so I'm about 7 hours in … I'm up to the Kumite/fighting now…not long to go!' It seems strange, but it helped me to get through, because I knew I could do it and that was the mental strength, borne through physical pain and endurance.

Chapter 7 – I Am Woman

I want to share with you now a blog article that I wrote back in 2013 entitled 'Pain and Gain'.

It's funny how you can think you know something for so long, perhaps almost your whole life, but then, one day, you live that thing and all of a sudden it all makes sense. The penny drops. Cha-ching. We've all heard the saying, 'What doesn't kill us makes us stronger', and I like the sentiment and have been known to throw that one around at various times but, in reality, the saying has flaws and can be used out of context. You see, things happen all the time in life that don't kill us, but neither do they change us. The things that do change us, which really do make us stronger, are those that push us beyond our normal limits, which force us to struggle. We must undergo difficulty in order to grow.

In nature, this could be compared to the process of natural selection. Those of the species that more easily adapt to the environment and overcome stressors and challenges survive. The strong survivors then breed and hence the growth of a stronger and more resilient population, herd, tribe, community, ecosystem or whatever term best describes it.

In the gym, or in training – referring to resistance based exercises, weight lifting, hypertrophy, power lifting, etc. – perhaps this is the basis for the SAID principle: Specific Adaptation to Increased Demands. Our body is smart and it has a memory and we are programmed to survive. Our very nature is to prevail, so when our body undergoes a stress, certain processes occur to ensure that next time we are better prepared.

Another way to explain it is that, very simply put, when we lift weights and apply stress to a muscle, damage occurs. It is through the process of rebuilding this muscle that the strength and size is gained. As a person, emotionally, when we go through hardships we tend to learn. We learn about how our mind reacts and we learn about our mental programming. We also learn that we can endure and that all things pass eventually and through this, we understand that we are durable and changeable and can weather a storm or two.

Next time, as we've been there before, we understand that the pain of losing someone, having an argument, being betrayed, being misunderstood, or perhaps being weak and hurting another person, no matter how bad it is, we can make it through, like we did previously. We recognise a pattern and can be stronger the second time around. We can make better choices this time.

The thing that I love about martial arts is that it covers all of the bases: our mental, physical, emotional and perhaps even spiritual aspects of ourselves. In one hard class alone we could touch on all these areas. We can challenge our self-beliefs like, 'I can't do another push up', and then you do, or thinking, 'I'm awesome!' only to get beaten in sparring that night. We can challenge our fears – our own inner demons – like, 'I don't want to spar this person – they're better than me', or, 'I'll never be able to last for that grading and survive it', and then we do. We can push ourselves so hard physically that we are in pain. We can demand of our body things that we thought we could never do, such as enduring an eight-hour physical grading or test with 40 x 1.5-minute rounds of hard contact sparring/

fighting, which is the requirement to obtain Black Belt in our style. And when we make it out on the other side our strength is resolved. Our mind is determined and our body is built that little bit better and we are more prepared to fight. Struggle is what makes us if it doesn't break us, but consider this: even if we are broken, just like our muscles after a heavy gym session, the right amount of love, medicine ('Let food be thy medicine and medicine thy food', so says Hippocrates), rest and recovery, meditation, sleep time, a small amount of will and drive, can restore us to be something better than we were before.

Consider, too, a hero. Every movie hero has a hardship. It's always the fall and then the rise and we love those stories. The loss makes the win so much more gratifying. We don't respect people who have it handed to them and often they don't respect themselves. So, knowing all of this, in the midst of your hardest training session, when you find yourself being beaten in the ring, when the odds are stacked against you, when you feel like you've been left with nothing, when you feel like you can't go on or get up after being knocked down, smile and remind yourself that it's moments like these (no, you don't need Minties!) that show you can and will survive and grow.

That's why I developed the I Am Woman experience, an 8-week fitness training program inclusive of body scans and photoshoot, which is really close to my heart. The I Am Woman packages differ from others out in the marketplace as the aim is not just changing the way the body looks from the outside, but focusing on the way the body moves, performs, and feels by developing strength both physically and mentally. It also has ME as the coach or facilitator which no other program has. J My goal is that I Am Woman sets more women on a path to finding their strength, setting better goals for themselves and understanding that they can do so much more than they think. You can find out more about the program at the end of this book.

Often, I see people begin exercise or training programs and then when the results don't come straight away and they're not getting the feedback they want or they're not seeing what they wanted to see, it's the time that they give up. The problem is, however, that some of these changes are taking place inside of our body and they're not necessarily visible to us or to others outside. What if you could see those? How would that change your exercise routine? Your motivation? If we can grasp that we are making progress and that positive things are happening, then this is the boost that we need to continue to keep going.

I Am Woman is there to remind women that the scales aren't your indicator for health or fitness or attractiveness. All a set of scales does is show your relation to gravity. It does not measure strength or height or your abilities or qualities. Scales are good for fighting weight divisions and for measuring cooking ingredients only!

I Am Woman is designed to focus on building form and function. When I say 'form', I mean form of movement and by 'function' I mean what your body can physically do. If you focus your training on trying to achieve a 'look', you will constantly be looking for flaws. When you focus on pushing towards a skill and a weight to lift or a punch or kick ... you see goals and you push harder towards them. Your body will change, but you will just be focussed elsewhere while it happens!

I Am Woman wants to show you that posture is queen! Film stars and models look great on stage and in photographs, etc. because they know how to carry themselves and how to posture to enhance their physical features. Postural correction should be a big part of any physical training.

Really, for me, I Am Woman means being proud of who you are and knowing your unlimited potential for love, strength, power and success. To me, it means accepting responsibilities and also having the confidence to say no when needed.

I Am Woman means being able to be all that you need to be for your loved ones, but also to yourself, and it's in acknowledging that in doing all these things, we will be perfect in our imperfection and that these nuances are what make us unique as individuals.

As you reflect on this chapter, remember this: You can be a mother, a lover, a woman and a warrior. You just need to be your own very best version of that. The one thing that nobody else can be that you can be, is you.

Osu

Notes

Chapter 8

Perfect Imperfection

Kintsukuroi: The Japanese art of repairing broken pottery with gold or silver lacquer, and understanding that the piece is more beautiful for having been broken.

I'm sure we've all heard the old adage, 'There's no such thing as perfect'. But what is perfect? In the Oxford dictionary, 'perfect' is defined as, 'Having all the required or desirable elements, qualities or characteristics as good as it's possible to be'.

In relation to ourselves and, in particular, in relation to us being a woman, or the perfect woman, what exactly does that refer to? I mean, who was it in the first place that told us what these characteristics, qualities or elements were in terms of a woman? Somewhere along the line, we decided these, I believe, for ourselves. Whether that was a result of reading magazines, or the person we idolised at school, or somewhere we've seen this movie star and we thought that's our idea of perfect, at the end of the day, nobody told us these particular things were perfect – we decided them on our own.

I believe in perfect imperfection. The concept that there are minor flaws in everything that makes it unique, individual and beautiful. Perfect imperfection is achieved when we redefine what the word 'perfect' means to us and understanding the difference between needs and wants in our lives and what fulfils us. When I'm talking about embracing perfect imperfection, I'm asking you to look at your rules and redefine them.

For example, you might consider that you've got rules about the way the house needs to be. You might want to have the carpets cleaned, the floors mopped, or the dishes done, the laundry folded. You don't want to have laundry out in the house. Nobody set these rules for you – these are your rules. Maybe they need to be relaxed a little. The house doesn't need to look like a magazine foldout during the day if it's causing you stress. If you're happy to do the work to make it look like that magazine cover then go right ahead, but if it's causing you stress because you can't manage it

Chapter 8 – Perfect Imperfection

or can't get it done, then maybe you need to reassess that expectation you've placed upon yourself.

I know for myself, especially early on when I had the kids at home and I was still trying to run my martial arts business, I was mainly teaching at night so I was home during the day and I had some rules of my own. I didn't realise I had them – they weren't written down anywhere – but I wanted the house clean when my then partner came home from work. I wanted the floors done, I wanted dinner on the table, I wanted the washing done and I tried to do all this with small children in the house, because I thought he'd be disappointed when he came home from work and would look at me in such a way as if to say, 'What did you do all day while I wasn't here?' I think the only time he ever said that was in jest, so essentially it was me who placed that expectation on myself.

Those were my rules and it used to create a lot of stress because I also had work that I needed to do for the business that didn't involve teaching. Paperwork to do, or emails to send, but I couldn't sit myself down at the computer until I'd done all of the housework and gotten the house to a level of tidiness that I deemed acceptable. And often I wouldn't actually get to sit down and do my business work, because I was unable to get all these tasks done whilst still having the kids in the house. How could I when they'd pull out more toys or mess up another outfit of clothing so again there'd be more washing and tidying, etc. I just couldn't ever get anything finished and I wanted everything done to completion.

Any woman knows that the housework is never done. So how was I ever going to achieve this perfect house when housework is never done, and there is no such thing as perfect? These were my rules and they were causing stress. What I actually needed to do was give myself a time frame. I had to say, between this time of day, i.e. between 9 o'clock and 10 o'clock I would have breakfast, give the kids breakfast, have a shower, get dressed and do all this essential household stuff. Give myself a list. Then from 1 o'clock until a certain time I'd sit down at the computer, get as much done as I could in that time slot and if I didn't finish everything, then that's okay – that task would go over to the following day. Then, of course, there's dinnertime and then getting the kids bathed and ready for bed so I could leave and go to the dojo once my partner had come home. I had to give myself blocks of times and relax the rules a little bit, because if I couldn't achieve in those time slots that I'd given myself the level of perfection that I was after, then I had to not worry; I just had to move it onto the next day.

That brings me to the next point about letting go. Sometimes you need to step back and get some perspective, and your children can be a wonderful and plentiful source of this. I remember one day when my daughter was doing something very suspicious over near the TV. I think she would have been about 3 years old and I looked over and said, 'Thaila, what are you doing?' She turned around and kind of held her hand up at me, like a stop sign and said, 'Mummy, go and do busy.' I was a little bit floored at that comment, because I knew exactly what she meant. She wanted me to go away and not watch her.

But it was the fact that she said, 'Go and do busy', that bothered me. These were my words! There were obviously times when she had in the past asked me to play a game, or read a story or watch a TV show with her, and I'd said, 'I can't – I'm busy.' And here she was, telling me to go away and do busy, because she didn't want me around. She was obviously doing something she knew she wasn't supposed to be doing, but it was the very fact that she turned around and my words were echoing in my own ears – that I'm too busy all the time – that was a bit of a slap in the face, because maybe I wasn't spending the time with her that I thought I was and here she was thinking I'm busy all the time. That's what I mean by perspective. That is a good motivator to change your behaviour, but doing so requires you to do some letting go. As I mentioned earlier, letting go is easier if you redefine your rules.

Something else that can help you to embrace perfect imperfection is to have a laugh. Try and see your shortcomings as humorous in a way, I guess. An embarrassing thing for women after they've had children is loss of pelvic floor and bladder control. You know … it's just not what it used to be. If you're embarrassed about it and you don't talk about it, you might feel like you're the only one going through it. You know you're not, deep down inside, but it can sometimes feel that way.

I'll never forget when I went and trained somewhere else, at a cross fit gym, and it was apparent very early that this was not a secret! In fact, there were a lot of other women there who would have a laugh about that. When skipping time came they'd announce to the coach, 'Oh, I've got to go up to the toilets and pee.' This meant we could all laugh along together. You need to be able to have a joke and laugh about these things, because if you can, it can lighten the load and you don't see things as bad as you thought they were.

Like I said, if you're failing to achieve some of these goals of yours, or you're failing to achieve this image of perfection, then maybe you just need to have a bit of a laugh, knowing that there is no such thing as perfection anyway and that it's okay to feel like you're less than 'perfect'.

People might say, 'What if I can't stand mess? I can't let go. I can't redefine my rules!' I would simply reiterate what I said before, that you really need to set more realistic goals. You don't have to accept that your house is going to be messy all the time. That's not what I'm saying. You just have to create kinder systems and schedules and be honest when you write them and enable yourself to be flexible with them. For instance, you don't know what's going to happen. One of your children could get sick, or you could get sick and you need to be able to say, 'Well, that's okay; I'm going to leave that x today. I'm going to be kind to myself and I know that within my schedule there's space.' Allow room in your schedule for the unexpected.

There may be those of you thinking, 'What if I just can't let go of these things that I want in my life?' Perhaps what you need to do is look at alternatives. Maybe you don't need to control everything – maybe you can give some of these tasks to your kids. Particularly if you have older kids, maybe you can delegate tasks and you can set up a list on the fridge or the wall and give rewards. It doesn't need to be monetary. If finances are an issue, it might be something like watching their favourite TV show or staying up an extra half an hour later – things that are important to the kids that make them want to do the task for you. They might not do them perfectly, but they might be done enough that it's okay for you in order to move on, to let go of the perfection. As long as the job is done, then it's done. Again, that's coming back to your rules and standards and redefining them.

I talked about trying to laugh at our shortcomings; however, there are some people who just might not find some of those things funny. Maybe we don't. The first time I experienced bladder leakage in a fitness class, the first time I went back to teaching and I was trying to kick and kick and kick, I remember feeling like, 'Oh, what is that?' I just had to deal with it on the spot, but went home and had a laugh about it later. I had faith that training was going to help it to get better. When something is embarrassing and you don't feel like laughing at all, or you don't want to tell anybody about it because it's not in any way humorous – at least not in that moment – remember you will learn to get better at it. Instead of getting upset at it, just breathe. If you can't laugh, then take a long deep breath and count to 5 before reacting. It sounds like a silly, basic thing to do, but often if we just pause for a few seconds and take stock, things aren't quite as bad as they seem. We're programmed to react very emotionally; however, by taking a few deep breaths, often things can calm down enough for us to find it amusing. Or if not, enough to let it go.

I've talked a little bit already about trying to be the perfect mum and the stress that comes from trying to do this. It's worthwhile remembering at this point that perfectionism is taught to children when they are punished for their mistakes. Maybe we, growing up, were chastised for our mistakes and because we were told we did the wrong thing, maybe we perceived ourselves as not being the perfect child, then progressed to not being the perfect girlfriend, the perfect friend, the perfect partner, the perfect anything. I think as mothers, then, we need to be aware of this. We don't want to say these things to our children that might lead them to this ideology in their minds.

Part of the concept of the 'perfect woman', I believe, is the ideal of the perfect body. I could spend a whole chapter on where this comes from … and the media and the movie stars and so on and so forth, but let's just agree for now that women are generally praised for their physical appearance from as early as babies and toddlers. There is still a very real underlying current that exists in our society that places a very high value on a girl's, and then a woman's, appearance, and what that should look like. I think we need to remember that if there is no such thing as perfect, then likewise a perfect woman cannot exist.

We need to accept this fact, because unless we do, we can't embrace it and if we can't embrace it then we can't do anything to stop reaching for and comparing ourselves to this ideal which isn't real.

I love this quote by Trent Shelton: 'Your flaws are perfect for the heart that is meant to love you.' Despite referring to something being perfect, I love this because what it's actually saying is that your imperfections are the very things that set you apart, and make you just right for the right person!

In terms of our bodies, it's nice to say that we want our body for ourselves, but I think part of us wants that body for somebody else. It's nice to have it for you – don't get me wrong, I want to feel strong and I want to be able to do certain things with my body in the martial arts – but I also want it to look physically appealing for the opposite sex, for my partner.

The idea of the perfect body is a complicated topic. Be gentle with yourself in that regard. I will elaborate on this topic in Chapter 12, but the last thing I want to tell you in regards to this is to stop comparing. Our biggest problem is comparing ourselves, and besides, just what are we comparing ourselves to, anyway? If you're going to compare yourself to anything, compare yourself to who you were yesterday. If you're not happy with yesterday, then every new second, every new morning, is a chance for a better you. A chance to do and be better than yesterday by embracing today.

Our quest, then, should not be perfection. It's about being the best you that there is. It's about striving for excellence rather than perfection, with excellence being the utmost we can be within our own parameters, and something that we can actually obtain.

Chapter 8 – Perfect Imperfection

If we can embrace perfect imperfection, then we will be spending less time trying hard to fulfil ideas that aren't achievable. We can also give ourselves fewer, or relax, our self-imposed rules. Let's be honest – who wants more rules? And if there are fewer rules or gentler ones, then we have more breathing space, more freedom. If we have more freedom, then we have more time to now devote to other areas of our lives. I mean, if we aren't spending all day cleaning the kitchen, there is time now to read a book or take the kids to the park!

If we can learn to embrace this perfect imperfection, then we are likely to be a more positive person instead of seeing ourselves as less than we want to be. We will eliminate negativity around not living up to unrealistic expectations, and remove unnecessary stress, anxiety, possible depression, a lack of self-confidence and possibly a lack of quality time with our children.

At the end of this chapter, I'd like to give you some exercises or some tasks that you should do to help you try to embrace perfect imperfection.

1. Write a 'like' and 'dislike' list about yourself, your body and your actions. It's about the way we are, the way we look, but also the way we act or behave. These are the things that make us who we are. Even though it might be confronting at first, have a go at it. You can use the table provided below … or, if you have a little book that you can write in and keep, use that. Just draw a line down the middle of one page. On one side write 'like' as a heading, and on the other, write 'dislike'. Jot down some things under each column. This is going to help put things in perspective of where you are and what things to look at, or what areas of yourself you might like to work on first. Be kind

but realistic with yourself as you begin to see things emerge onto the paper. Just splurge and try not to overthink.

2. Next is to make a 'wants' and 'needs' list. When you've made these two lists, your likes and dislikes, then your wants and needs, I want you to reflect on the two lists. Try to discover where these attributes you believe you have, e.g. your likes and dislikes, are coming from. What, too, are these wants and needs stemming from? Look to see if they are hinging on some self-imposed rules that you have created. If you can identify where they're coming from then it's possible to change some of the negative traits or let go of them if we realise that they're coming from a place that doesn't serve us anymore. Likewise, if there are positives, think about how they can be nurtured and cultivated to turn good into awesome!

3. Next, think about how, if you could change your rules, would your new list look? Write yourself this new list. Can you see yourself in the future once you've changed some ideals? How does that make you feel? Amazing, right?!

4. I encourage you to have a read of Perfectly Imperfect by Connie Howell. As I was writing this book, my kids demanded to be taken to the local library one day. We went along and I thought I'd use the opportunity to do some research of my own. Browsing the shelves of the self-help section, I spied this tiny yellow book in amongst the large selection of books. I'm not sure why I was first attracted to it, but there on the spine was the title: Perfectly Imperfect. I just had to borrow it. It was so timely as I had just written this chapter. I sat in

the park while my kids played in the sunshine that day and read about half the book. I then finished it later that afternoon. Immediately, I contacted the author to say thank you as it was such a fantastic read. I also requested permission to recommend this little book here as further reading, as it ventures far deeper into the topic and offers a lovely and unique perspective.

Good luck!

Osu

Likes	Importance 1–5	Why do I like this?	How can I capitalise on this?
Eg: My sense of humour	4	Can make people laugh	helps me see the funny side of mistakes or when things go wrong

Dislikes	Importance 1-5	Where does the dislike stem from?	How can I change or accept this?
Eg: My temper	5	Regrets from acting in anger…… my kids faces	Practise meditation, Don't rush and place extra pressure on myself so I don't have to get angry

Chapter 8 – Perfect Imperfection

Wants	Why do I want this? (be 100% honest)	Do I need this Y/N	Number in order of priority – describe action plan
eg: To be more muscly and stronger	It will make me feel strong and as though I have achieved something in my training	N	3. Be more consistent in my training.
Needs	**Why do I need this? (be 100% honest)**	**Still Need ? Y/N**	**Number in order of priority as above – describe action plan**
eg: A new car	Because current car is breaking down and becoming expensive. I also think I deserve one.	Y…soon	4. Start a savings plan. Maybe $50 per week

Number your priorities from 1 (highest) to 6 (lowest) priority. Give the things you need a higher priority. Work through your list in order of highest to lowest priority and work out an action plan!

Notes

Chapter 9

Because You're Worth It!

Life is short. Buy the shoes.
– Anonymous

During the social revolution and the new rise in feminism in 1973, Ilon Specht broke new ground with a contemporary ad for L'Oréal, which ended with the signature phrase, 'Because I'm worth it.' Then, in the mid-2000s, this slogan was changed to, 'Because you're worth it.'

This slogan, then, has been the calling card of this massively successful company for over 40 years. It's such a strong message and a powerful ad campaign because it gives us permission to indulge ourselves in fine and/or seemingly extravagant things, whilst assuring us that it's okay despite our underlying doubts that we are worth it. Worth the luxury, worth the time and the monetary spend. The need to feel worthy is so powerful and such a driving force that it is one of the six basic human needs as identified through psychology, originally by American Psychologist Abraham Maslow. The need to feel special and significant is one of those basic needs.

Initially, this chapter was going to be called 'Pamper You', but I struggled to write it. It just sounded wrong and I didn't want to say the old tried and tested line of, 'You are a priority, so you must look after yourself in order to look after others.' And not because it's not true – of course it is – but because that's not where the problem is.

I realised that there is so much in life that we know is good, or correct, or the right thing to do, but something prevents us from doing it. For example, most people know that they need to eat healthily to keep their own good health, but they don't always do it. It might be because they don't think they have time to prepare the meals that are healthy, they think it's too expensive, or they just don't enjoy the food as much and hence choose otherwise. Usually these choices are justified somehow, but are mostly untrue if really analysed and considered.

Conversely, people know what they shouldn't do and still go ahead and do it regardless. For example, knowing that smoking is unhealthy and linked to cancer and yet choosing to smoke cigarettes anyway.

As I have said before, it's about the why. Why you should pamper yourself occasionally. I'm not saying be irresponsible and lavish yourself with shopping and expensive spa treatments, but that we all need to feel that we are special and that we are worth it. If, once a month, we are needing to get our sexy back by having a wax and a facial, then by all means we must allow ourselves to find a way.

Knowing that you need to have a massage, or get your hair styled, or have a night out with the girls reminds you of your own self-worth. Making the time and scheduling these activities, treatments or whatever it is you feel that you need, is signifying that your time is important to you, so that you value your own time and, therefore, choose how and where you spend it. It also shows others that your time is important and if you keep telling yourself and you keep repeating, 'Oh, I can't because …' or, 'I shouldn't because …' you're just reiterating that to yourself and those around you.

Remember, this becomes our own internal dialogue and this is the stuff that we subconsciously refer to. If an offer to x comes up, if our internal dialogue is constantly telling us, 'No, you can't … no, you shouldn't', this is almost going to be an automatic response, and that kind of thinking is really hard to break, and affects us in many other ways. It's not about just pampering yourself, but it's about that inner feeling of worth that's going to then impact everything else we do and everything else that we deserve. There's that saying, 'We get what we deserve' – and when you consider that closely, that means you get what you think you deserve and maybe it's time to change what you believe you deserve and what you believe you're worth.

You might say, 'Oh, I can't afford it … I can't afford this treatment … I can't afford to pay to get my hair done at the salon … I can't afford a massage.' They seem like big expenses, but maybe you can't afford not to! Now is a good time to really look at where you spend your money. Are you often doing costly activities with the family instead of free fun like the park? Are you buying toys for your kids because you want to provide so you want to give it to them? Are you using excess power at home by using the clothes dryer for convenience … or other things like these seemingly small purchases that add up? Is there somewhere that you're spending your money unnecessarily, but you're choosing that over yourself because you don't think you're worth it?

Perhaps it feels selfish – that there are more important things – and I just want to say, 'Really?' Because I'm pretty sure that your own happiness and your mental health is important and should be high on your list of priorities. Again, remember that your kids and your friends and everyone is watching and learning from you. Your kids are witnessing how they should treat themselves and you are teaching friends and family how to interact with and treat you by the way that you treat yourself. If you don't feel worth it, I really want you to revisit that thought, and I suggest that you need to go back to the previous chapter and look at the table with your likes and dislikes. You need to ask yourself why, because you are worth it. We all are.

At the end of this chapter I really just want you to do one main thing:

5. Rephrase your thinking. If you're constantly coming up with reasons for why you shouldn't treat yourself, then maybe you need to change that to, 'Why shouldn't I?' It's going to be hard at first, as these things become an internal dialogue and it takes a conscious effort to change it but, after a while, like everything else that we do repeatedly, it's going to become a habit. Hopefully, you can change that unconscious talk to yourself into something more positive.

Osu

Chapter 9 – Because You're Worth It!

Notes

Chapter 10

Designing Destiny

Watch your thoughts; they become words.
Watch your words; they become actions.
Watch your actions; they become habits.
Watch your habits; they become character.
Watch your character; it becomes your destiny.
— Lao Tzu

Rome, they say, wasn't built in a day and I doubt that it was constructed without a plan, either. This is the chapter where we get to the often considered boring, but grossly undervalued topic of goal-setting. I can almost see and feel you wincing, hearing this word: goal-setting. I'm sure you've been at work meetings, or attended conferences, entrepreneurial seminars, wealth-building classes or read self-help books and, if so, I'm positive that in all of those there was a section regarding the importance of goal-setting.

We hear that and think, 'Oh my gosh, I'm going to have to sit down and write these plans and make up stuff that I don't believe and will never follow through on', and I don't want this to be a chapter like that. Here is where my old school sensei streak comes out and where I get out the shinai – the bamboo stick – and give you a bit of a whack and say, 'Come on – try a bit harder. It's all up to you. Wake up!'

Now's the time to accept responsibility for your future. Your destiny is nobody else's problem but yours and though other people can help, at the end of the day it's up to you. It's your choice. It's your actions. It's your dreams. Your destiny. Yes, life is a journey to enjoy but you have no cause to complain if you don't like your destination at the end if you don't go to the trouble of planning your trip.

How do we know where to start? I'd say that if you sit still long enough and search within yourself, you know. We all know. It's just all the rubbish in our head – the doubts, the insecurities, other people's opinions, our inner dialogue, our subconscious stuff that makes us believe that we can't do things – that falters us and causes us to second-guess and question whether or not we can achieve our dreams or our destiny.

Napoleon Hill, a famous philosopher who wrote a book called Think and Grow Rich, said that 'a goal is a dream with a deadline'. It's important to have dreams, but without setting a timeline on when we would like to have achieved these things by, then they most likely will remain dreams. Setting measurable goals is imperative for us in terms of shaping our future and designing our destiny.

I don't want to give you a long-winded plan. I want to give you quick and simple ideas or steps that are easy for you to slot into your lifestyle. It's the little things that we do every day that ultimately add up to the bigger picture, the

Chapter 10 – Designing Destiny

end result. Aristotle can be quoted as saying, 'We are the sum of our actions and, therefore, our habits make all the difference.'

Yes, there is a little bit of stuff to do at the outset, but don't you think your future is worth it? It's worth a few minutes of your time … or an hour or two, or, indeed, however long it takes because, in the end, what price do you put on your happiness and success? Really, if it realises your dreams, it's not even a sacrifice.

My lucky number is 6. I thought it would be auspicious, then, to give you 6 pointers that I believe can help you to shape your destiny.

1. Just start. The first thing you need to do is to make the decision to plan and create change. Everything in your life starts with a thought. You cannot do anything actively without first thinking to do it. It's important that you know what you want and decide to obtain it. You know in your heart this is true.

    If you look back on anything that you really, really, absolutely had to have in your life so far … did you get it? I know that I did. And if I didn't … then I guess I just didn't want it bad enough, or I gave in due to letting my doubts and insecurities take over. Look back over time and be honest.

    My eldest son is a marvel at making things that he wants appear. It might sound silly … but, for example, he will want a specific toy car. He will ask me at the shops and I will say no. So that's when he goes into planning mode. 'But, Mum, if I earn enough points' — which he gets by doing chores or good behaviour — 'can I use them to get the car later?' I will say yes. So then, at home, he will find the toy catalogue where he initially saw the toy and circle it in pen. That will stay in his room. Then, pretty much every day, he will remind me as he does something good or earns a point that he is getting that car.

Eventually ... like magic ... he has it in his hands. In my life, growing up, I knew how to get the stuff I wanted. Maybe it was a pair of fluoro socks ... Mum said no, but I knew if I worked on Nan a little bit she would eventually cave. Later, as I got older, things got harder – Nan couldn't always get me that job or promotion – but I would always find a way. But ... only if I believed I had to have it and if I believed I could do it. I wouldn't stop trying till I succeeded.

2. Don't focus on every little step; focus, instead, on goals. If you sit down and write a long list of steps, it's going to look daunting and you're not going to want to go through with it. The steps will often reveal themselves as you go along and you keep your eyes forward on your desires, your prize. I've heard that a great thing to do is to visualise yourself achieving those things and try to imagine how you feel when you have accomplished them.

It's amazing that when you do focus on the destination, things have a way of occurring or coming into view that take you to your next step. Then the next one. You don't need to worry about all the steps, as they will happen. You just have to keep your eyes forward. Stay focused and trust that you will see the next step once you scale the one you are on. Indeed, you must take action, but focus on the big tasks and the larger plan. The goal is what keeps you going, what drives you forward.

3. Try to implement or do something daily (or at least weekly) that will get you closer to your goal. If you miss a day, don't chastise yourself. Sitting there worrying about the fact that you didn't do something is only going to lead to negativity and self-doubt, and will perhaps mean that in the end you'll give up. If you do miss doing something, if you've promised yourself to complete a particular task, or set a target to achieve that day and you miss that for whatever reason, just push that over and make it a task for the following day. Continue to move forward with your plans.

4. Be the ball. There are times when you get on a roll and the best thing to do then is just go with it! When you've got motion, when you've got momentum, stay with it, keep going … and going. Use the energy that's created in the positive motion to keep moving, keep edging forward towards your goals. This is also the time to watch for bad habits jumping back into you. It might be fear of either success or failure that could stop you and cause you to regress. When I say fear of success, I refer to when, perhaps, you start to see things happening, you start to see things changing, and you get afraid and say, 'Oh my God, am I going to be able to handle this? I'm getting all these new clients, all this new work, and I don't know if I'm going to have the time to do it all. How am I going to manage? What am I going to do when I get this many people?' Well, do you have that many people yet? When the time comes and you need to make a decision or you need to find a way, you'll find a way. Don't be afraid of your success, don't be afraid of growing – this is ultimately what you want to do and it will just be a little bit scary when it starts to happen. Be the ball!

5. Be observant. Watch for coincidences and opportunities disguised as luck. The Roman philosopher, Seneca, once said, 'Luck is what happens when preparation meets opportunity.' I believe he is not saying that there isn't luck, but that we create our own luck. When we're focussed and we're driven and we're out there trying to achieve, things that will help us reach our goals inevitably turn up in our lives and if we are looking for these things, we'll notice them and say, 'Oh, that was lucky … That was a coincidence, and arrived right when I needed it.' It probably would have turned up anyway, but had you not been focussed, had you not been looking, it would have just passed you by and you would have not noticed it. Was it coincidence? Was it luck? Or were you meant to get it and was it just the fact that you were prepared that you saw it?

    While you're observing and monitoring, keep tabs on your successes and your losses and start to notice patterns. If you need to make changes to strategies because they're not working, then change them. If you notice things that are working and are getting you success, these are the things you want to grow or continue to implement. Observe, measure and adjust!

6. Make a vision board. This is a good old-fashioned tool, but it's just so useful! I'm talking about getting a big corkboard, a canvas, a picture frame – whatever you want to use – it doesn't matter. You need something you could hang up in front of your desk, or in your bedroom, or in your bathroom – somewhere where you're going to have to see it all the time, because we want to keep the things that we want to achieve in our focus.

If we think about something or keep ideas in our mind long enough, we eventually bring that thing into our being. It would make sense, then, that if we're going to manifest these things into our lives, that it should be something positive, something that we desire to have in our life. So, make a vision board. If you want to envision yourself living in a particular style of house, then find a picture of that house and stick it on your vision board. If you'd love to drive a certain type of car, then get a picture of that car and stick it on your board too. If there's a particular quote or an affirmation that you want to remember and you want to try and say this to yourself as often as possible, stick that on your vision board. If you want a particular piece of jewellery, but you can't afford it now … if you want to have a massive family and are struggling to conceive again, then maybe Photoshop some kids into a picture or cots or beds, put up photos of yourself pregnant, or make invitations to your baby shower. Stick that up – something that's going to remind you of these things you want to achieve and keep it in your focus. Keep reminding you of that all the time.

And … definitely include the Lao Tzu quote from the start of this chapter on your vision board!

What are you waiting for? Time to get started, time to make some decisions, time to write some goals, time to take action, time to go out and design your destiny.

Osu

Notes

Warrior

Fighting

My heart beats loudly in my ears, almost bursting through my chest.

The time is now; it's time to see who wins and who is best.

It's down to just the two of us – we're standing toe to toe.

Have I trained enough for this, I ask. Well … soon we'll know.

The doubt – it starts to creep inside my mind; it almost hurts.

My body turns to jelly – shit! … then numb … Don't know what's worse.

I try to psyche myself up, but it's like there is no use.

Still … there's no backing out of this – no treaty and no truce.

I turn my mind inside – remember why it is I'm here.

And then, from somewhere deep inside, there's this roaring in my ears.

Sounds like a lion in the jungle or a pack of Samurai

as they emerge through forest thick – attack and scream their battle cry.

Perhaps the crowd is what I hear – but, no, it's something else.

That noise is what it sounds like when you murder fear yourself.

Now adrenaline is pumping and the room shrinks half its size.

I'm down at one end of a tunnel; at the other end's my prize.

But my prize is not a trophy. No, it's not a piece of tin.

All I want is justice. Pride. Respect. I just really want to win.

Chapter 11

Warrior Training

We are what we repeatedly do. Excellence then, is not an act but a habit.

– Aristotle

I was 19 years old and after a tumultuous 5-year relationship I was dumped. I still remember that night and the following morning and the lead-up to it. I knew that there was another – a blonder, prettier, slightly older – version of me with more money, who was my replacement. We even shared the same name and that didn't help. I think that made 3-4 of us now – Kileys, that was!

It just felt so awful, so horrible, that there he was breaking up with me and I was begging him not to, even though I knew I'd been cheated on again. Of course, I see the irony now. It should have been me leaving him, right? Me saying, 'How could you do that? Nobody treats me like that. I deserve better.' And that's just it – I had no confidence left in myself then. Nothing made me feel worthy or strong or proud enough to stand up for who I was.

Off I went to work, dejected, feeling sad and desperate. I had to hold back tears most of the morning and somehow perform my job, which then was in a warehouse at a large printing press company called Heidelberg Australia. In that area of the company, I worked mainly with males, so nobody I felt I could really bounce my feelings off. As the day wore on, I realised I was feeling worse and worse and I remember thinking that this can't be right. I was upset, but this was ridiculous. So at one point, when I had taken to the sanctuary of the women's bathroom yet again, I noticed it. The red spot. The fever. And oh, I was itchy. Great. Chicken pox.

As if I wasn't already beside myself, I now had to look at my spotty and scabby little face and body, and stay at home quarantined with my misery and dwell over the shady position I was now in. Perfect. Just perfect.

During this time at home, somewhere between the oatmeal bath and dabbing on the calamine lotion, I had a realisation! I asked myself what would I do anyway if I wasn't stuck at home? Which friends would I be out with and what would I do? Because, come to think of it, I had made his life mine and I had kind of lost contact with all of my friends and my life was really his. I spent so much time at his place and I didn't have any hobbies of my own. That's when it dawned on me. Please forgive me because I was only 19, but as silly as it may sound, I thought, 'I'll show him!' He had been involved in Zen Do Kai, a martial art style, and now I was going to do it.

But I was going to do kickboxing and be better at it and get back at him. I'm not sure why I thought it would even matter or that he would even care, but I'm so glad I did think this way at the time or else my life may have turned out so much different. I guess, really, now that I think of it, I should

Chapter 11 – Warrior Training

thank him. I suppose, like they always say, everything does happen for a reason.

Grabbing myself a Yellow Pages, if you remember them, I scoured through the martial arts section and saw an ad for Eltham Martial Arts Academy. It was a bit of a hike as I wasn't a local – it was probably a 30-minute drive from my house – but to me it looked the best. They also offered karate and the ad was nice and big and … I don't know, that's just the one that caught my eye. I called up and was told I could come and get a gold pass, which would let me try all the classes I wished to for a week. I wanted to start straight away, while the iron was hot and before I chickened out.

I was very shy back then and it took all my courage to drive my little Mighty Boy (that was my first car), down to the dojo, which is what we call 'the training hall' in Japanese. On that first night, when I got there, I sat in the car park for a while, trying to will myself to enter the building.

Finally mustering up the strength, I walked into the reception area and even though I had originally chosen to do kickboxing, the first class of the week was karate and I figured I'd give that a try. Why not? I was there. Even though I felt awkward, everybody was really friendly and it just so happened that the head instructor, George Kolovos, was teaching the beginners' class that night. He wasn't always there for that session, but this particular night he was.

Well, I loved it and I never looked back. And I can't say for sure what drew me to karate, but I never did try that kickboxing class – at least, not until a few years later. It will sound crazy, but that night I just knew … it was a feeling or connection that this was something I was supposed to do. For the first time in a long time, I had a sense that I could actually be good at this. I got to yell and kick and punch and I was going to get strong. I just believed it.

I felt empowered already. Not because after one class I could actually perform anything that resembled a technique, but I was on a path and this time I felt sure that it was a good one. After commencing my practice of Kyokushin Karate, it soon became an obsession. I was starting to miss late university tutorials, because I didn't want to forego a training session. I was desperate to move from the beginners' class into the intermediate. Their class was on after the beginners' session, so I'd often stay back and watch the second class and just be in awe.

I was, of course, impressed by everyone, but I remember being amazed by Sempai Serina. She became my inspiration. Her technique was flawless; she was so disciplined and committed and at training every night. She seemed to know all the terminology, the katas (certain choreographed techniques and movements formed into a pattern or routine) and was small and fast and agile. Here was this younger girl, a little like I was, who was clearly advanced and I wanted so much to be like her.

I was really surprised that, as well as Serina, many of the higher ranks and instructors were females. I don't know why I was surprised, but I was. Perhaps I just didn't expect it.

There were also two other instructors who visited the dojo to teach – Sempai Maria and Sempai Elica who were both very strong and tough and commanding. I had heard that Sempai Maria was a full contact fighter and had competed internationally and I was super impressed. I thank my lucky stars to this day I walked into that dojo with such a high calibre of instructors and role models and especially that there were such strong female leaders to be inspired by.

Very soon, my training became a six-day a week regime. I was training at Eltham, the city and Moonee Ponds dojos during the week, and on Saturdays I would attend Eltham in the morning and then drive to the city for the afternoon

Chapter 11 – Warrior Training

sessions. Life for me became so much about karate and 21 years later I still have no regrets. Sure, I had fun and I socialised and went out, but more often than not I was like, 'I'll drive – I'm not drinking as I'm training for a tournament', or, 'I can't go out; I have training in the morning', or, 'I'm tired from training.' Most of my socialising, then, was done with the karate crew and it usually involved eating after classes or tournaments or gradings, and the occasional sayonara (goodbye/breakup) party or camp.

My longest friendships have come from my involvement in martial arts and it's definitely grown to be my life's passion. So, at this point I just want to say, Mum – you were wrong. When I first told her about joining karate, she brushed it off with an, 'Oh, you just want to meet boys; you won't stick with it.' Anyway, without making this section a 'This is my Life' story, I can't tell you enough how it really did transform my life.

There are so many good stories I could retell here in relation to my experiences in karate … but that would constitute a whole other book. What I do need to convey, though, is how at my innermost core, I know how much of my strength and resolve comes from my martial arts training. The word 'osu', which you have been repeating on your way through this book, comes from the Japanese saying, 'Osu no seishin', which roughly translates as 'the spirit of perseverance' or 'to persevere under pressure'. It iterates the development of a steadfast mindset that never gives up. One must endure under adversity. The word 'osu' is the shortened form of this saying. At the dojo, whenever we greet somebody who's a higher rank, a fellow student, we bow and say, 'Osu.' When given an instruction or command during training, our response is always, 'Osu.' It is said quickly and firmly and loudly in class. Osu is a sign of respect, a signal that you have heard and understood, but on an even deeper level, when you say it, you're promising to try and push and to do your best. To never quit.

We say it so much that, to me, it's become ingrained. Indeed, I have left business meetings at work and, upon leaving the meeting, turned, bowed, said, 'Osu', and then realised, slightly embarrassed, and just kept on walking, hoping that nobody noticed.

That's how training works. If you repeat things enough, if you say them enough, if you're inspired enough, then these habits become imprinted onto your very personality and onto your soul. Showing respect to others becomes habit. Politeness, courtesy – these are things instilled in your psyche through martial arts and, better than that, through the hardest of training and pressures I've learned that I'm so much stronger than I ever believed.

I know that I can be pushed till I want to vomit and keep going. I know that I can do 9 hours of hard training and fighting and survive. I know that I can lose a fight and it's not the end of the world. I just need to keep training and get better and stronger. You can't win them all. I know that if I try I can stay cool under pressure. I know that I can be nervous as anything and not back out or back down because I don't really want to. I've known the taste of victory and I like it.

I know that no matter how much I know, there is always more to learn. I know that Black Belt is just the beginning. I know that training is a journey where you never reach a final destination. Like life, once you stop travelling and learning, it's over. I also know that if I fall, all I have to do is stand back up. All this I know and developed through my Kyokushin training.

Kyokushin means 'the ultimate truth'. Now, at first this sounds like an arrogant statement, meaning that Kyokushin karate is the best. But, indeed, that is far from the truth. I believe that Sosai Mas Oyama, the father and founder of Kyokushin karate, chose this name because he believed that in every training session we should search for our own truth. The truth about our character, our will and our inner resolve. We are all in search of our own ultimate truth, of our inner fighter. I do believe that inside all of us is a warrior; it just needs to be trained.

It's a funny thing to think of oneself as a warrior. I, for one, know that I'm not the best fighter, or the strongest, and I'm far from the biggest. I'm not the best martial arts instructor either, I'm sure, but I'm passionate and I'm proud and I have pushed myself as hard as I can and I've spent more time on the competition mats or sparring in the dojo than many. Do I think that I'm a warrior? I've been called one on occasion and hearing it brings up seeds of doubts in my mind. I've not won a world tournament, so how can I say that? Then I think, 'No, I am a warrior', because I've fought so hard for so long to keep teaching and training, under so much pressure sometimes, but never did I give up.

Warrior training or training of any sort, I believe, is imperative for self-development because it pushes your boundaries. It stretches you and improves you. Joining a training group of any sort will also give you another social outlet and aspect in your life. It gives you a new circle of friends – people whom you have really strong connections with – and often these people you're with all the time have the same mindset and understanding of things that you do. Even though they're different, there is still that similarity that keeps you together as a group and as a community.

Any sort of physical training, I believe – will improve your confidence and it's definitely going to improve your fitness and health. The bonus of martial arts is that it has the advantage of being self-defence, so fitness with a purpose. I've heard that slogan used as a sales pitch before, and I think it's a great statement conveying the benefits of martial arts.

One of the greatest benefits of physical training is that it helps give you passion and purpose. Over my time, I've attended numerous seminars, weekends and educational meetings pertaining to health, business, wealth-building, and so on, and in every one – and it's not an exaggeration; I mean literally every single event – at some point they'll talk about the importance of having passion and purpose. There are plenty of studies, too, that you can reference for examples (you only need to jump online to find them), with regards to the importance of passion and purpose. As a general list, these studies tend to show that having a sense of purpose helps you to live longer, protects against heart disease, helps prevent Alzheimer's disease, gives you more resilience and higher pain tolerance and, of course, gives you better relationships.

If you're missing out on this physical training, this warrior training, and if you don't have this fitness and passion and health and purpose, then your life can't possibly be all that it could be. You can't be all that you could be and you will suffer in some ways and particular areas of your life will be less because of it.

The Macquarie Dictionary defines a warrior as 'one who is engaged or experienced in battle or warfare'. It also describes a warrior as 'fearless and courageous in support of a cause or an issue'. Not everyone is going to sign up to fight in the army or jump in a tournament arena, but you can still be a warrior.

My instructor would always say that it wasn't the fight that made you better, not the grading or the test, but it was the training you did in preparation for that event. I say, therefore, that it's what you do on a daily basis. If, every day, you train to be a fighter, you train to be fit – to push yourself beyond limits, to go on when your body cries 'stop' and to stand up when you want to fall – your drive is to be the best that you can be and so that is your passion. That is your attitude and that is how you behave and then, I guess, that is who you are. You are your purpose.

Perhaps every day your job involves driving an hour to work where you're a chef and you cook for people because you love it. Your work is a drain on your social life, you're away from your family at night, but you struggle to make it work, because your favourite thing is to watch people enjoy the creations that you've made for them. That is your drive and that is your passion and you endlessly pursue it and you fight to maintain that lifestyle instead of giving into what's easy. Then you are the chef warrior.

For those of you reading this who wonder, 'What if martial arts isn't for me?' – it might not be for you, but unless you try it, how will you know? I believe martial arts is for everybody and there's something to be found in it that helps everyone – young, middle-aged to older people. It's about choosing the right one for you. There are so many different martial arts to choose from. There's even gentle martial arts; tai chi, in its basic form, comes from martial arts. An older person, as well as a younger person, could quite easily partake in tai chi. Tai chi's fantastic. What I'm saying is that you don't have to do an aggressive form of martial arts. There is something for everybody and, as I mentioned, the advantage of it is that you do obtain the self-defence skills alongside all the other benefits.

What if somebody were to say that they've tried martial arts, but they don't like it? I'd say, that's okay. Your training doesn't need to be martial arts. I love martial arts, but yours doesn't need to be martial arts. I do think, however, you need to find a sporting activity or hobby which gets you moving. Yoga, rock climbing, obstacle racing, walking the dog … whatever it is, just find that thing you love that gets you moving and pushes you, and do it religiously. Do it daily. Sosai Oyama used to say, 'Train more than you sleep.' For most of us, I think that's an impossibility. But train often. Train as much as you can.

What if you say, 'I don't know what my passion is'? Well, that is why it's so important to try new things, to make time for you. You likely do know, if you really sit with yourself for a while. You will know what your passion is, but maybe it's just not a priority right now and other things are taking over. Somehow you need to make it a higher priority, you need to bring this passion, bring this purpose back into your life. Like I said, it's great if it is something that's also going to get you fit and healthy as well.

But continuing on from that, it doesn't need to be something that you like and you can indeed be impassioned about something, or trying to right something, that's wrong in the world. You might campaign in your spare time for ethical treatment of animals … anything. The thing which bothers you in life is, I guess, not your job, but maybe that's the thing in life that you're supposed to achieve or strive for. It frustrates you enough for you to do something about it. You're driven to do it; you're passionate about it and that is part of your purpose.

Maybe, like I said, it doesn't need to be something that you really 'enjoy' doing so much as you're passionate about it. If this is the case … I still want you to pursue health and fitness. Having a fit and healthy body and mind is without question the backbone to being able to forge ahead in your quests elsewhere.

Wrapping up this chapter, I want to give you some to-do points:

1. I want to stress to you, please find your passion and purpose. If you've still got that little book that we've used a couple of times, please grab it out and just brainstorm – start writing down all the things that you love. It's important for so many reasons that you do this and it doesn't matter if the idea or thing you're passionate about is crazy; you need to not worry about what anyone else thinks and you just need to write it down.

Chapter 11 – Warrior Training

2. Please, please, please, have a fitness regime. Try new things. Don't get stuck in a rut. Our body needs to be placed under different stresses to adapt and change as it's how our body grows and gets stronger and evolves. Survival of the fittest. We have to adapt to stay strong, so if running is something you enjoy and that's going to be your fitness regime, that's fantastic, but maybe there are other things you'd like to do as well. Definitely do your running if that's what you're driven to do, but every now and again go and do some swimming or try something else. Maybe if you're sick of jogging, you might want to look at a marathon or do some sprinting within your field. Try new things. Keep it fresh.

3. Do something that challenges you and do it often. Ensure it's physically and mentally challenging and taking you out of your comfort zone.

Osu

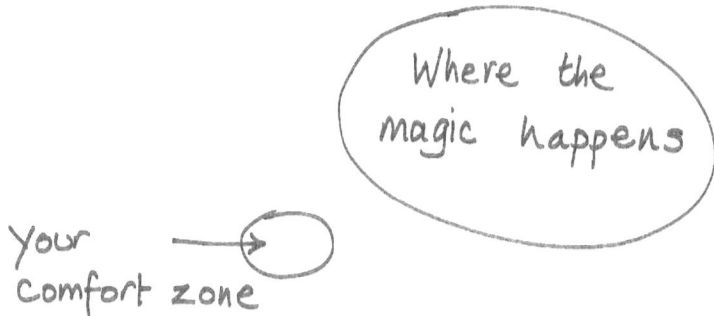

Notes

Chapter 12

Who's in Your Corner?

Surround yourself with the dreamers and the doers, the believers and the thinkers, but most of all, surround yourself with those who see the greatness within you, even when you don't see it yourself.

— Edmund Lee

Any time that a fighter steps onto the mats or into the ring, they want to have a good team in their corner. These people know them, have trained with them and know how to help them to win. During the round, when the fight gets tough, when they're feeling under pressure, they can listen out for the voices calling instructions from the corner, telling them what to do. Often, from the outside, they're there looking at the fight and seeing things that we can't see when we're in the thick of it.

In the breaks during the rounds, when the fighter goes back to the corner, the team is there. The trainer or chief second jumps into the ring and talks to the fighter. They tell them all the things that they're doing well, but also points out the things they need to do better. There's the second (the other corner person) with the ice pack on the back of the fighter's neck, cooling them down, giving them a sip of water if they need it. They may be rubbing the fighter's shins, looking after them, and preparing them to go back into battle. They're there for support and they're there to ensure victory, or to help ensure victory as much as is possible, for the fighter.

Isn't life the same? We all want to win and we all want to be a success, so it would then make perfect sense to have around you a team of people that are helping you achieve. When it comes to our families, we can't really choose who they are. If you have a really supportive family full of great role models, then consider yourself very fortunate. If not, you might not be able to trade them in, but you need to just love them for who they are, and perhaps choose to limit your interactions with them and control the amount of influence they have over you and your decisions.

Friends, colleagues, partners, etc … we do have control over the selection of these people. Great mentors and business coaches will talk of surrounding yourself with the people whom you want to be like, whom you aspire to be like and are already achieving what you wish to achieve.

Basically, what I'm saying is that you need to build your winning team. The benefits of having your own winning team are that you're surrounding yourself with positive energy. Your team will keep you focussed on the good things and they won't bring you down so there will always be this feeling around you that good things can happen.

You know, yourself, if you attend an event such as a party, you could leave and say, 'Oh, that party had a bad vibe. It wasn't a good feeling. The energy wasn't great.' You want to surround yourself or put yourself in an environment as often as possible where the energy is great, where you feel good. If you have a winning team, then you can learn faster from the lessons of those that have gone before you and if you're doing that, you can save time and you can save energy. If you've got a team around you, then you have a network of like-minded people. This creates opportunities and magnifies coincidence.

When you want to quit, when things get tough, somebody is going to lift you back up, give you a helping hand and a pep talk, and push you back in there and tell you to keep going. Alternatively, sometimes forging ahead in the wrong direction is not always the smartest move. If you look like you're making a bad decision, perhaps one that someone on your team has previously made themselves … or you just look like your head isn't above water … then maybe they will throw in the towel and rescue you. They'll cover you and help you save the good fight for another day. Basically, they'll have your back.

If you don't have that winning team around you, then there's nobody in your corner, and you'll be almost going solo. Without their knowledge and advice you'll be spending more time trying to figure out things they could have already told you. Your health may suffer without their guidance and treatment, and you may be working harder (not smarter) for less reward. Worse, if you have a losing team, then everyone's just going to keep on pulling you down to keep you down with them.

What exactly do I mean by a 'winning team'? First, you have to pick your priorities and then find your guru for each one. For instance, one priority might be health. You can have a look at whatever health treatments are out there for you. There's osteopathy, chiropractic, myotherapy, acupuncture, massage, homeopathy … there's a broad range of treatments and care out there for you that can see you on a path of good health. You will want to choose which practitioners to see for which health-related concerns you have.

Career and business mentors … that's another area you might want to have a look at as part of your team. These are the people who are already doing what you want to do within your chosen field. Someone who can tell you the mistakes that you've made and what not to do and they can steer you in the right direction, because they've got experience.

A possible third position in your team is somebody who's going to help you with your fitness. Health and fitness are closely linked, but they're not the same thing. Do what moves you. Choose something or someone that's going to motivate you and push you and move you from the inside and out and, at the same time, someone who's going to support you during that. The fourth position on your team could be friends and kindred spirits.

So, who are you going to choose to fill those positions? There may be more. You might have other priorities. As I said, the kids and your family … you can't choose those, but be very selective when you begin picking your team. Over time, I've had different problems that particular practitioners couldn't fix. After I had quite a bad car accident when I was in my early 20s, my neck had whiplash. I had massages, I tried stretching and ice and heat and all those sorts of things but, at the end of the day, it wasn't until somebody suggested I go and see a physiotherapist that I went. Now, the physio that I ended up making an appointment with did therapies like ultrasounds and cupping and stuff that I hadn't seen before, but he was also a manipulative physiotherapist and used manipulation techniques whereby he adjusted my back. The instant after having the adjustments and ultrasound treatments, my problems started to go away. That physio treatment was a great solution and I was glad I tried it. I also believe it put me on the path, actually, to seeking out chiropractic treatment and osteopathic treatment later down the track.

There was another pivotal time, too, after I had my first child. Being in the martial arts, I was very quickly back into fitness and I was stretching and kicking and trying to get back into my training. However, every time I tried to kick I was experiencing extreme pelvic pain and it was progressively getting worse. For me, that was a big thing because it was limiting my work, my hobby and my goals and so I really needed to get this fixed. I saw doctor after doctor and I was eventually referred to a gynaecologist. I don't know why – the problem did not feel to me as though it was gynaecological because it was a very deep, internal pain. Nobody else could tell me what was wrong, though, and as the doctor suggested, I thought I should still follow through with the exam. Right before I was due to go to this appointment, a friend suggested osteopathic treatment. I hadn't tried that therapy before and, being open-minded and at my wit's end, I sought out this osteopath and, although she told me that it was a hard problem to fix, she was the only one who was actually able to correct that. I never did need to visit that gyno specialist.

Having gone down this path, nowadays if I have a particular weird issue with my body then often chiropractic, osteopathy or myotherapy will be the first types of treatment that I go and seek, but it was a process that took me there. Is my neck out? Okay, I'm going to go see my chiropractor. Do I think there's muscle tension and something that's affecting one of my joints and causing me problems? Right, I'll go and see my osteopath or my myotherapist. If I damage or hurt myself and there is an injury that requires attention, it's reassuring having those people in my team whom I know I can call and trust, and know that my health will be looked after by them.

Many people refer to these types of treatment as 'alternative' health care. I have also used the services of my homeopath and naturopath when required, and I actually don't believe they are alternative at all. Perhaps 'complementary' is a better term. I mean … what's the other option? Your local GP? Your General Practitioner is, I guess, covered under Medicare or your chosen private health scheme, but I don't believe them to be the only source of health care available. They are also not specialists (thus the name General Practitioner) and I would prefer to cut out the middle man and go straight to the healthcare professional that is trained in the area of expertise that I require. I am not saying they don't have their place – but, like any other service, you go where is appropriate.

What is also great about treatments such as massage or naturopathy is that they can set you on a path of returning to and maintaining optimal health. A masseuse can help prevent injury by keeping your body tension-free, and you feeling relaxed. A naturopath can provide nutritional plans and long-term strategies to keep you well, which may include addressing sleep issues, allergies, and possibly the effect of emotional issues on your health. I just don't think that GPs can offer that level of service and it feels to me that often, it's just in to the examination room … a few questions … then a prescription along with the side effects and a short-term solution. I have very strong opinions in this area, and it's not the book to address them all, but it's something for you to consider.

You could be thinking you can't afford to constantly be visiting these practitioners. You don't, however, need to go and see them all the time. This is something that you do on a 'need to' basis or set yourself a maintenance schedule you can manage. If you're extremely active, then massage may be something you want to try and find time for semi regularly if you're often really pushing your body to its limits.

It might be your job that is placing your body under a lot of stress, if you're a brickies labourer, or a builder, or a nurse where you are lifting and moving patients and on your feet all day, or something like that, or you're moving heavy things around all the time. You really need to look after that body of yours. At the end of the day, if you don't look after your body, you can't turn up for work.

You might feel that you can't afford it, but can you afford not to? What price do you put on your health and wellbeing? What else are you finding money for that you don't need to? Do you smoke cigarettes? (You should address smoking for other reasons also!) Do you buy alcohol? Do you buy take away coffee? Are you buying lunch out every week? There is always stuff that we spend our money on that we don't need to. Or that we shouldn't because the money could be better spent elsewhere. I'm not saying never do that. I'm not trying to tell you to never drink, but just asking you to look at where you're spending your money and make sure it is going to give you the most benefit and is in line with your priorities. Health should definitely be up there on your list.

In regard to your friends, one thing we need to do is analyse our circle of friends and whom we associate with on a regular basis, and we have to ask ourselves questions such as, 'What is similar about my friends and me?' 'What sort of things do we talk about?' 'Are we discussing things that are going to improve us, that are driving us forward? Or are we constantly complaining about how bad our lives are and how little money we have and how our car's broken down and is it a negative environment to be with these people?'

I'm not supposing that you don't sometimes discuss negative things with your friends. I mean, they're the people whom you bounce this stuff off, who are there for you and comfort you and help you through hard times. That's not what I'm saying. I'm asking if, when you get together in a group environment or one on one, are these people providing positivity on a regular basis?

As a rule, are these people doing well? Are they striving for more? When you spend an amount of time with these connections, do you walk away feeling energised? Or do you walk away feeling drained? Do you walk away feeling good about yourself and your dreams and aspirations that you've discussed and they're encouraging you? Or do you walk away feeling like you've just had the wind removed from your sails?

It's imperative that you analyse your circle and you need to be very honest. Sometimes, it can be really hard if they're long-term friends and deeply entwined in your life, or even family. Maybe it's not an option to eliminate them from your circle or your life, but perhaps you need to distance yourself from them a little bit and limit your interactions and also put up some barriers of sorts when you're talking to them. You know, end conversations if it's going in a negative direction, agree to disagree … ultimately, you need to look after yourself.

If your friends aren't wonderful and they aren't driving you forward, then make new friends who are. Here is where your social network, your training places and fitness groups come into their own where kindred spirits can be found. Make new friends at these places!

In regard to your career and business goals, talk and network. Don't clutch all your cards to your chest. Tell people what you want. Tell people what you'd like to be achieving and

Chapter 12 – Who's in Your Corner?

where you'd like to go. Talk about your ideas; for the most part, you don't have to keep everything a secret. When you do talk about ideas, you'd be surprised at what networks you create and within those, there'll be coincidences. Look for them. Coincidences aren't all they appear to be. They're opportunities, so take note and see what turns up because I think you'll be surprised.

What do you do if your partner doesn't want you to succeed? If you're feeling like your partner's the one who's not in your corner and not on your team, then you really need to bring them on board. You've got some very serious talks that you both need to have and some honest communication needs to occur. You need to stay calm, you need to be clear and you need to be truthful and specific. You really, really want to get them on board and you need to show strength. I'm not talking about aggression; I'm referring to strength. Be strong enough to put across your point of view and explain why it's so important to you and also why it's really important for you to have them on board and how that can also benefit them.

In closing this chapter, I will set you this one important task:

1. You need to choose your winning team. You need to write down or, at least, consciously choose who you need around you for what you want to achieve. Remember, the winning team isn't always the one stroking your ego. They will always tell you the truth. They will never say you can't do something, or try to belittle you, or put you down. Sometimes they'll push you well out of your comfort zone, but when they do, they'll always be there by your side, supporting you. Happy Choosing!

Osu

Notes

Chapter 13

It's Not About the Belt

The true essence of the Martial Way
can only be realised through experience.
Knowing this, learn never to fear its
demands.

– The 10th Motto of Mas Oyama

We keep hearing that life is a journey and it is the experience which is to be enjoyed. Stop and smell the roses, and appreciate where you are for exactly that moment. Live in the now. But we are also then told to focus on goals and look ahead into the future. All the advice we are getting then seems somewhat contradictory. Live in the now … be present … set goals … make a vision board … take steps every day towards your dream … Well, isn't that looking forward and not being fully present?!

On the surface, I suppose that's what we are being asked to do, so it's understandable if it's confusing, but it doesn't need to be. You need to be able to do a bit of both. To keep a foot and your conscious mind in the present, but your subconscious and your mind's eye on the future.

I guess what's important is that we do keep our end goals in mind, whilst enjoying the process of achieving them. It's this state of mind, where we can be happy knowing that we are moving in the right direction and heading towards our dreams and appreciating that in the now without worrying about the completion date – that is, the ultimate aim.

You see, at the end of the day we do want to attain or achieve certain things, but it's not by the acquisition of 'stuff' or obtaining the 'end result' that we find ourselves changed and fulfilled. Being presented with my Black Belt did not shape the karateka (karate practitioner) that I am today, nor the instructor or the fighter. Even the grading test itself, though arduous and pretty much 9 hours of mentally and physically exhausting training, techniques and fighting, wasn't what made me into the Black Belt, either.

It was the work and training I underwent each day, each week, each month and each year that made everything else possible. It was all the gradings I had endured prior to the Black Belt one that made that a reality. You cannot skip steps. You mustn't go in unprepared or you will be broken in a grading like that.

I still remember the pressure leading up to that day. Once I put in that application form I had made a commitment – a pledge to myself, to my instructor and to the other members of the dojo. Now, I could not back out or else, to me, my word was broken and, therefore, my honour gone. I'm not talking about trying and failing and losing face. No. To fight and fall is still a victory. I'm talking about losing honour if I didn't have the courage or conviction to follow through with the grading. That was something I couldn't accept for myself.

Chapter 13 – It's Not About the Belt

I know many people have undertaken this test. It doesn't require a person to be superhuman. In itself, I guess, it's no extraordinary feat … however, to those who have gone through a Kyokushin Black Belt grading and done the 40 rounds of contact fighting … it's something to be nervous about. It's one of the reasons why Kyokushin doesn't have the greatest number of Black Belts in comparison to other martial arts, and the reason why it takes, on average, around 5 years for most to achieve. It's a long-term plan.

Having witnessed previous Black Belt gradings as I was moving through the ranks, I knew what I was up against. I had seen good and bad results. I had seen the student get kicked … slump against and then slide down a wall … only to be pulled back up to their feet and kicked back down again. It sounds vicious, but it's more about fatigue at this point than being hurt.

I had seen people not know katas, or forms, properly, or know them but be so exhausted that they just lost it on the day. I didn't want to do any of that. I knew I'd have a tough time, but I wanted to perform to a high standard on grading day. My instructor had asked me to take part in the grading as he thought I was ready, despite having only recently achieved the rank before, being 1st Kyu. Because of this, I didn't want other members of the dojo to talk badly of me if I didn't do a good job.

Having made the decision to grade, it was now time to kick the training up a notch. I was already training almost every night – only now with renewed focus and energy. I had also begun running on my work lunch breaks. I really dislike running, but it's great for building stamina and this was one thing I was going to need in bucket loads.

At this point, I was working at a company in Richmond, and the best part was that the run was along the banks of the

Yarra and it got me out of the office for a while and out into the sunshine. My boss, a friend (RIP R. Bannister), and a few other guys had a regular running club and I asked to join in. I ran hard – as hard as my tiny legs would take me – and I'm competitive so I pushed … but I pretty much got my butt handed to me by the old blokes every run. It's funny now, but at the time there were days when I just thought, 'If I'm getting beaten by these guys with at least 20 or so years on me, am I even fit enough?'

Then there was the karate training. I'm not sure everyone has the same experience, but there were days when I would question that I even knew much at all. It probably doesn't help when your instructor yells it at you, either! I still vividly remember the night when a group of us were getting ready for a grading and we were training at the Eltham dojo. Sensei Kolovos was putting our small group through basics, and I'm not really sure what I did wrong … or if it was, in fact, me … but he gruffly asked us what we thought we were doing trying to grade when we didn't even know how to do Jodan Uke' properly. (This is one of the first blocks you would learn in your first class!) Maybe that was a way of messing with our heads, getting us to try harder, be more critical of our basics … but it certainly made me question myself that night.

The idea of the 40 fights hung over my head like a storm cloud in a cartoon. I wasn't worried about the repetition of basics and stances for the first few hours. I wasn't concerned with the katas, which roughly took another 35-40 minutes. I thought kata was one of my strong points. I was slightly hesitant about the Ippon Kumite (single-step fighting sequence in which you have to show a number of different techniques without repeating any) and whether I would just all of a sudden go blank or mess up my order. I felt the same regarding San Bon Kumite (three-step fighting with

Chapter 13 – It's Not About the Belt

takedowns and/or restraints). I wasn't wary of the stamina, either. Yes … as if the grading wasn't enough of a test of stamina, there were also 100 each of push-ups, squats and sit-ups. I knew that all I had to do was keep pushing and those would get done. The written test didn't bother me at all. I was pretty much okay with my terminology and knowledge of the tournament rules and wording, etc. The board-breaking was on my mind as I hadn't done that much before … but I was okay with it.

I will admit now that I was afraid of the fights. I wasn't afraid of getting hurt. I knew already that was going to happen and that the pain would pretty much come later anyway when all the bruising and swelling came out the next day. No … I was worried that I wouldn't do well enough. That I wouldn't be able to hold up and still be fighting back when things got tough after the 20th or so round. That I would basically turn into a punching bag.

So, the Friday night fight class took on new meaning. It was time to start getting conditioned and learning how to just move, pick good shots and keep going when exhausted. There was a smaller group of us that would do extra training before or after class, or on Sundays, etc. and we would just fatigue ourselves with running or sprints and burpees, then proceed to just do round after round after round on the bags. I don't think you could really replicate the grading in your training. You can, however, prepare your mind and that's what I tried to do to the best of my ability.

I was extremely nervous the night before and on the morning of the grading. I tried to calm myself with the grading day ritual I had evolved over the years. This meant washing my dogi (uniform often referred to as 'white pyjamas'), and ironing it, then folding it up in the traditional way and tying my belt around it. I washed and packed my mouthguard. Everything needed to be clean and packed properly. Then

I organised my snacks and drinks for the day.

My tameshiwari (technique for breaking concrete tiles, timber boards, or ice) boards were now packed after having chosen them carefully, storing them in a dry place and airing them out to make sure they were ready for breaking. I also spent time the night before going over and over my Ippon Kumite techniques and anything else that worried me.

When grading day finally came, I felt ready. That morning, I woke up extra early. I think the grading started at 10am so I had to allow enough time for myself to eat a large and healthy breakfast and for it to digest. I had to force the food down. Eating when you are nervous is not ideal. Bacon and eggs, muesli and yoghurt and some OJ was my pre-grading meal. I had also 'carb-loaded' the night before. It was time. I was ready and waiting for my lift to arrive. You can't drive yourself to a Black Belt grading. You won't be driving home.

Suffice to say, I survived the grading and managed to get through the 8 hours of training, testing and fighting. It was tough and there were times when I mistakenly looked at the clock and thought, 'Will I make it?' There was sooo long to go and we were still doing Ido Geiko (walking basics). It sometimes felt like repetition, repetition, repetition and if the Black Belts running the grading said 'Ura' (performing techniques where you spin around first) one more time ... I was going home! (Never ... but I was pretty sick of spinning in Ura.)

To be honest, I don't remember much of the fighting. It's always a rush of adrenaline and you get a second wind when the kumite (the actual combat fighting) starts. It's a change of pace with no more thinking and concentrating on stances, etc. It's time for sparring. The fun part, normally, and the time when you know the grading is drawing to a close. But that's when you see all the fresh-faced Black Belts in their

Chapter 13 – It's Not About the Belt

unsweaty dogis who have come out of the woodwork just to see you endure, and to help put you through the torture they had to go through themselves.

It's a special time, in an almost sadistic kind of way! We all show each other respect, but that respect is by hitting you just enough to make it worth it – make you earn it – without sending you to the floor in a puddle of yourself. It's easy to hurt someone who is physically, mentally and emotionally fatigued. So, the hits are strategic by the Black Belts. They hit you just enough to almost drop you … then they encourage you to fight on. To an outsider, I guess it could look a little barbaric. To us … it's an honour.

I was so drained and just so thankful when the buzzer went at the end of the 39th fight. One more. Just one more. And then … it was done. Looking at the 'after grading photo', I can see myself and the other Black Belts are so gaunt-looking, like we had been starved for days. It just takes so much out of you. I know people who have had to go to hospital afterwards. It's not uncommon. And these aren't ill-prepared or unfit students – these are really strong, fit men who really go hard and give their absolute best and their absolute all. Yep, the grading is tough.

At the end of my Black Belt grading, I didn't cry. At least, not that I remember. Previously, I always did, though … right up to my Brown Belt. It's common after a long and demanding event to shed a tear of relief once it's all done and dusted. It's like you have been strong for so long … given your all … and now you can stop. I'm still not sure why I didn't cry this particular time, but I put it down to training and preparing for so long and thus being more prepared, but also just being that physically exhausted after that I really didn't have the energy to shed a tear.

The grading, though, is merely the test. The test of

everything that you did, and all that came before. It's the way to see if you are now ready to start learning karate. The old masters say that Shodan, or Black Belt, is the level which signifies you have mastered the basics. You are now ready to begin the real journey.

The black belt itself didn't make you ready, though. The black belt is just the thing around your waist that holds the dogi jacket closed. The belt is to be respected, of course, but not for its magical powers. It has none. What's special about the belt is what it represents. It represents the hours of training, and the blood and sweat and tears that went into earning it. It represents the knowledge you have garnered and the time you have dedicated and sacrificed. It represents your commitment and honour to your style.

It represents overcoming obstacles. Sometimes those obstacles are external but, for the most part, I think those hurdles are things within ourselves that we have to get over: doubts, fears, lack of confidence, limiting beliefs, distractions and perhaps our ego. The Black Belt is the White Belt that never quit, so it represents a spirit of perseverance and a 'never give up' spirit that we each hold proud in our hearts.

I'm telling this particular story because I want so much for you to remember that although we think obtaining something will make us great, it won't. What makes us great is what we endure and learn on the way to achieving it.

For example, if it's a Porsche 911 (my son's dream car at the moment) that you desire, there are a number of ways you could get this car. You could a) steal it, b) win it in a raffle or c) work your butt off and get the money to purchase it. You will feel great driving around in that car and owning a luxury vehicle … but how different do you think person a) will feel as compared to person c)? In their heart of hearts, person c) will know how hard they have worked. They will see so much more value in it, and not only that, they have acquired the skills to get another one if they wish. Sure, person a) could go steal another one … if they aren't in jail … but how do you think they feel in their heart? Nobody truly values something they get for free, and it doesn't make them a better person.

Another example is the fighter, the champion with title belts or trophies galore. Depending on the sport, they may also have a large purse to show for them. However, when we see this person, what do we really value? Is it their money? Is it the awards and accolades? I don't believe it is. I think we respect them for their skill and mastery of the art.

For their courage and conviction and their heart. The trophies or the ring or mat time didn't give them that. The hours spent training while their friends went out socialising did. The diets, the bruises and the 5am starts did. The hours training in the shadows while others basked in the limelight did. The money they spent on their coaching and their gym gear and their travel and their novice fights did.

We must remember all these things while we are working towards our idea of victory. In the hardest moments when we want to quit, or think we are failing, we need to remember that these are the best times. These are the moments that make us great. They allow the victory to happen and we need to enjoy it then and there. And if we truly can't enjoy it, we can respect it enough to know that it will, indeed, bring us the happiness we deserve if we just don't give up.

In Kyokushin karate, we have an oath, or Dojo Kun, that we recite at the end of every class. It is our sign-off after each training session and a chance for us to pause and reflect on our efforts that day. It's also a reminder to ourselves about keeping our focus and our principles.

Mother Lover Woman Warrior

I have created a Mother Lover Woman Warrior oath for you:

- I choose to accept the challenge of life and vow to win.

- I will remember that I am stronger and more capable than I know.

- I will strive for excellence and improvement daily, remembering my aim is perfect imperfection.

- I will always remember I am important, I am needed, I give love, and I am loved.

- I will aspire to be mindful of the present moment.

- I will never quit until I am satisfied I have reached the destination of my dreams.

Chapter 13 – It's Not About the Belt

Notes

Afterword

Sometimes, it's not the workout that matters.

It's the turning up against all odds. Fighting the excuses. Pushing through a hard day and showing up to class, the gym, the Dojo anyway in spite of the adversities.

It's about putting on the gloves, or picking up that weight or running that track when you don't want to.

When you feel like you can't and then you do.

It's the fight.

The struggle and the overcoming of adversity that makes it all worthwhile.

That's when you know you can push yourself harder than you ever thought possible.

That's when you win.

This is where you show the universe you are serious and you want that thing more than you want to feel comfortable and then your victory is imminent.

Actually, you've already won!

Go for it. Kiley xx

About the Author

Kiley Baker is a single mum who runs her own martial arts academy, Eltham Martial Arts Academy, where she teaches and trains clients 6 days per week in both martial arts and general fitness. It is her passion to empower and instil strength, fitness and confidence in all of her students, and especially to reach out to other women such as herself.

Kiley has three children: Thaila, 10, Deshan, 7, and Sanjay, 4 years old. She obtained her Black Belt in Kyokushin Karate in May 1999, Second Dan in December 2001 and, after having her three children, was graded to rank of Third Dan in December 2013 by her instructor, Shihan George Kolovos, as part of South Pacific Independent Kyokushin. The rank of Third Dan was also recognised by Shihan Judd Reid and Chikara Kyokushin Karate in December 2015. In November 2003, she was awarded the rank of Instructor as a part of Titans Kickboxing Academy, a representative of ISS Thailand.

Kiley is a five-time Victorian Kyokushin Champion, winning her division in 2001, 2002, 2004, 2010 and 2016. She is also a three-time World Ring Karate Australia winner, including the WRKA Bantamweight title in 2002, as well as having competed and placed at both National and International events.

Kiley's passion for teaching and passing on knowledge began in 1998 when, as a Brown Belt, she started teaching the beginner Karate class in the Melbourne City Dojo. As her love of Karate and the Japanese Culture grew, she secured a job in Japan teaching English. However, just before heading off to Japan, she was offered the role of head instructor and manager for the Eltham Martial Arts Academy which was then under control of Shihan Kolovos. After a fire destroyed the club dojo in 2000, the opportunity to take over the dojo was offered to Kiley. She moved it to the local Research Primary School Hall and Eltham Martial Arts Academy took on a new lease of life. The dojo remained at the school hall up until 2007, when Kiley made the jump to a full-time dedicated centre, and opened at the Academy's present-day location.

Kiley is a qualified personal trainer, obtaining her Certificate III in Sport and Recreation in 2002, and then Certificate III and IV in Fitness in 2012/2013, respectively. She is always on the lookout for new ideas in relation to health, fitness and a holistic approach to both of these. Kiley can often be found attending another martial arts seminar or trying yoga, Crossfit, and other training modalities in an effort to keep her knowledge fresh and interesting, and also just for a new challenge.

I Am Woman

What's Included	I AM WOMAN JUMP START	I AM WOMAN ADVANCED	I AM WOMAN VIP
Customised Body Scan x 2 (Start & Finish)	✓	✓	✓
'Bellatrix' Female Warrior Classes (2 per week)	✓	✓	✓
Mother Lover Woman Warrior 'Book'		✓	✓
Personal Training Sessions		1 per week	2 per week
Personalised Program Creation		✓	✓
Fortnightly Mindset Workhop/Session (30-60mins)		✓	✓
Resistance Band		✓	✓
Access to the I Am Woman Secret Facebook Group			✓
Success Journal			✓
Foam Rehab Roller			✓
Unlimited Laser Phone Calls			✓
Photoshoot & Pamper Session (incl.2x proffessional prints)			✓

SPECIAL BOOK OFFER
TRY A WARRIOR SESSION
WITH KILEY

Would you like to try a martial art, but are too scared to attend a class?
Are you bored of your current fitness regime, and want to try something new?
Do you need to build more strength of body and mind, and grow your confidence from the inside out?

Undertaking a new physical training regime can be daunting and difficult, but with the right support it really can be life changing. If you would like to see how the I Am Woman package works without having to sign up for the whole program this could be a great way to start!

Claim Offer Email Kiley @ Elthammartialarts@gmail.com with subject line SPECIAL BOOK OFFER or phone 0410 603 464 !

Special Book Offer Only

You get Initial Consult and Assessment

One Hour Personal Training Session

Take Home Training Program for your fitness Level

Valued at $100 your investment only $45

Kiley's websites

motherloverwomanwarrior.com

www.justwordsnotpoetry.com

www.thinkmartialarts.com.au

www.elthammartialarts.com

Find Mother lover Woman Warrior on Facebook !

KILEY BAKER
As a speaker

Kiley Baker is the Author of the book Mother Lover Woman Warrior, a business owner, successful martial artist, personal trainer and mother of 3 children. Her passion is to inspire other woman such as herself, to pursue their dreams and achieve all they desire by discovering their inner strength and worth through fitness and the development of a positive mindset. This was the basis for the development of her 'I Am Woman' 8 weeks to Warrior Program.

Having been instructing for over 20 years, Kiley has had experience in coaching both children and adults from 4yrs - 60+ yrs old, males and females alike and loves watching people grow and change through their training.

Her own experience in the competition arena and sending students to compete internationally gives her a unique perspective when it comes to personal training and the mindset surrounding ones physical fitness.

Kiley is a sought after speaker on the following subjects:

EMBRACING THE ART OF PERFECT IMPERFECTION

- *Balancing motherhood with your passion*
- *How you can do it all*
- *Understanding why sometimes it's not you ...it's them*

INSIDER STORIES FROM A FEMALE WARRIOR

- *Why martial arts is great for women*
- *Being ferocious but feminine*
- *The power of mindset in creating a magnetic presence around you*

CREATING A WARRIOR MINDSET

- *How to make decisions not excuses*
- *Creating champion habits*
- *Finding and focusing your 'why'*

" Great Corporate Packages including Mindset Mastery and Board Breaking "

CONTACT INFO: 0410 603 464

www.motherloverwomanwarrior.com

email : elthammartialarts@gmail.com

Online training videos

Access to secret social media group, and network

Weekly information and coaching kits

Weekly Phone Mentoring

I Am Woman Warrior Kit

ONLINE
EDITION

Want to experience the I Am Woman Program from a distance?

If you would like to partake in this package, but are unable to travel to its location, then let the program come to you!

Train when and where you want to but still get the same advice, training programs, mentoring and information that makes the program great.

CONTACT US FOR
MORE INFORMATION

elthammartialarts@gmail.com
Ph.: 0410 603 464
Motherloverwomanwarrior.com

www.ingramcontent.com/pod-product-compliance
Lightning Source LLC
Chambersburg PA
CBHW020424010526
44118CB00010B/410